In a Strange Land…

In a Strange Land...

People with Dementia
and the Local Church

a guide and encouragement
for ministry

Malcolm Goldsmith

4M Publications

First published in Great Britain in 2004 by
4M Publications
20 Dover Street
Southwell
Notts. NG25 0EZ

British Library of Cataloguing in Publication Data
A CIP catalogue record for this book is available from the British Library

ISBN 0 9530494 6 9

Produced in Great Britain by
MD Print & Design
Edinburgh

Contents

This book is dedicated to

my friends and former colleagues

Mary Moffett

&

Douglas Yeoman

who so ably and compassionately

minister to people with dementia

Also

with gratitude to the Trust

which enabled this work to be

researched and published

ACKNOWLEDGEMENTS

I would like to thank the many people whose works I have briefly quoted or referred to. Their work continues to provide a solid base upon which further imaginative structures of dementia care can be erected. I have referred often to Richard Cheston and Michael Bender's most informative book *Understanding Dementia: the man with worried eyes*, but also to many other works.

Monica Furlong's 9 lines of the poem 'A Slum is where somebody else lives' in *God's A Good Man* (1974 Mowbray, a Continuum imprint) are printed with permission.

Extracts from *The Book of Common Prayer*, the rights in which are vested in the Crown, are reproduced by permission of the Crown's Patentee, Cambridge University Press.

John Killick's poems from *You are Words* and *Openings* published by Hawker Publications (Books) are quoted with permission.

Extract from *Common Worship: Pastoral Services* is copyright © The Archbishop's Council 2000 and is used by permission.

I have endeavoured to give due acknowledgement to all quotations used, but have been unable to track down all the information needed on Judith Scott (page 107) and Barbara Beuler Wegner (page 167).

I am indebted to Professor Mary Marshall and staff at the Dementia Services Development Centre in Stirling for their support and guidance over the years. I am pleased to say that for every book sold a donation will be given to the DSDC.

Finally my thanks go to Marion for her constant support and encouragement when the going got tough, and to my colleague and friend Anne Brotherston for all her administrative and secretarial support without which this book might have remained a pile of papers on the floor.

Foreword

It was said of my namesake when he was the British Prime Minister that his besetting sin was that he believed in the innate goodness of humankind. It can be said of Malcolm Goldsmith in the writing of this book that his great virtue is his passionate belief in the innate goodness of God.

God is the umbilical cord which sustains every human being. God is there when all that seems left of a person is an empty shell, a caricature of what it means to be a person. For the author, this is not just faith in the face of evidence to the contrary. He has learned this from experience and from over forty years as an Anglican priest. He has stories of parishioners who at the point of death and in a near vegetative state respond to a prayer with an 'Amen' or with some other affirmative response. He has learned that in the transaction with a person with dementia he can meet God. "I believe that there is no-one of whom it can be said that the Spirit of God cannot penetrate their troubled mind".

It is upon such faith and experience that the pages of this book are written. Indeed we are privileged readers for there are not many people who write about both spirituality and dementia. Malcolm has researched, lectured and published on dementia for the past ten years or more and it is a testimony to his communication skills that he has been able to synthesise this with his understanding of spirituality and religion to give us this accessible practical guide.

Combining the academic and the practical, dementia insights and theological conviction, he explores the person-centred approach to dementia care and provides a resource for shameless plundering and referencing by carers and for those of us who have, or have had, relatives with dementia and who want to hang on to the person and address the person rather than the illness.

Malcolm meets the challenge of this head on. For him, the person with dementia remains a person up to the point of death. That person is sanctified ground, whether he or she is in hospital, in residential care, in church or at home, and however lost the former self seems to be. As carers we have to develop our personal resources to treat them as such.

This book has been salutary reading for me. My mother-in-law died recently with multi infarct dementia, after living with my wife and me for several months before being admitted to a Christian nursing home where she was well cared for. She died contented, with my wife by her bedside.

My own mother had Alzheimer's for more than ten years. For half this time she lived with my sister and her family but for more than six years the illness was chronic and precipitated a move to a nearby nursing home. My sister was the principal family carer and visited her almost every day. The toll on her was great, and to this day I believe that the worry contributed to her getting cancer and dying at the young age of fifty-nine. I realise now that the visits I made to my mother were sporadic, partly because I lived over three hundred miles away, but also because I no longer saw her as a person. Atrophied to the foetal position, she was incapable of sight recognition, of speech, of sensory perception and she depended totally on her carers for her every need. I could not see beyond the 'body, brain and breath'. On several occasions I was tempted to give her a big hug and a kiss and to place a pillow over her face with the words: "Good night, God bless, mum". I never did, but was appalled when summoned suddenly to her side in hospital when she was thought to be dying, to discover my sister trying to feed her to keep her alive and arranging that she be given antibiotics to fend off a 'flu virus.

Today I realise that my sister saw our mother as a person, whilst I saw her as a non-person, a mere shadow of someone who had died years before. Had I read this book then, I might have been able to see my mother as the person that she still was, and this would have enabled me to play my part more fully, visit her more often and also relieve the pressure on my sister.

This experience may be familiar to some of you. You too may think "If only . . .". But we cannot live in the past and one of the many strengths of this book is that it helps us deal with our guilt and with our weaknesses in the face of dementia. We learn that we too are loved by God in the same way as those with dementia.

The Psalmist asks "How can we sing the Lord's song in a strange land?". This is both the challenge and the opportunity for the carer, whether a relative or a professional and for the person with dementia. The book answers with a: "Try this". We are given a whole raft of ways to write a new song which gives dignity to all concerned. We learn about the positives of an early diagnosis, how to understand and communicate better with those who have dementia and how the churches can adapt and make accessible their message both to carers and to people with dementia. We are given prayers and reflections at the end of each chapter. The book is a mine of information and of practical suggestions - a must for every church congregation, residential home or family where there is dementia.

Over time churches have adapted to make provision for women, for people with different coloured skins, for those of different cultures and orientations. There is now legislation to make buildings accessible for those with physical disabilities, and every church must have a Handbook on Child Protection. Perhaps the time has now come for every church to have a book such as this in order that no-one, but no-one, is left alone and forsaken in that 'strange land' of dementia.

Of course this book is not prescriptive enough to write a definitive 'song'. But it does offer us many tunes which, if used, will give dignity to the increasing number of people, including ourselves, who have or who may develop some form of dementia.

It was Martin Luther King who wrote words which Malcolm could just as easily have written: "When our days become dreary with low hovering clouds and our nights become darker than a thousand midnights, let us remember that there is a great benign Power in the Universe whose name is God, who is able to make a way out of no way and transform dark yesterdays into light tomorrows".

Neville Chamberlain
Bishop of Brechin

Introduction

How shall we sing the Lord's song in a strange land?

The purpose of this book is to affirm and facilitate an awareness that people with dementia are unconditionally held within the love of God, and that it is part of the calling of the church to minister to them with sensitivity and compassion.

It is written primarily for church leaders, be they lay or ordained, in the hope that it might encourage and support them in this difficult and demanding area of ministry. I hope that it will also be of support and encouragement to those who carry the burden of care, whether within a family or a professional capacity. Finally, if it can offer any words of hope to people with dementia themselves, then I shall be profoundly moved.

The text draws upon the insights and work of a great many people; that is quite deliberate. I want to demonstrate that there are now large numbers of people who are committed to exploring and honouring the experience of dementia. It is an invisible community of care and concern, whose desire is to ease the pain and confusion that is invariably associated with dementia, and to offer greater understanding and encourage good practice in diagnosing, standing alongside and caring for people with dementia.

I have endeavoured to give full references, so that those who wish to might extend their reading and follow up particular points in greater detail. However, the text can be read straight through by ignoring the referencing system.

One of the problems that anyone faces when writing about dementia is the fact that we are focusing upon an illness or disability that can affect someone over a long period of time, for perhaps fifteen years or so although usually not so long as that. This time span covers the progress from normal health through until death. It is therefore very difficult when reading about someone with dementia to know just whereabouts on that time scale the person might be located. The early period may last for five years or more, during which time a relatively normal and reasonably independent life can be lived. Later periods however, will see the person severely cognitively impaired and needing a considerable amount of supportive care. So there is a sense in which to write about 'a person with dementia' can be a very loose and generalised thing to do, in reality, telling us very little. Added to this is the fact that no two people are the same, nor are their circumstances and patterns of relationships. Great care must therefore be taken and the limitations of language understood, accepted and allowed for.

In describing where we are in Dementia Care I often suggest that it is as though we are facing a vast ocean and we have only just begun to step into it and get our feet wet. It is my hope that this small book will give us the confidence to take another small step forward into the ocean of the unknown. Because I write from within the community of faith, I dare to believe that stepping out into the unknown is often a characteristic of discipleship:

> and it's from the old we travel to the new
> keep me travelling along with you.

Words from a hymn by Sydney Carter, who was himself to travel into the strange land of dementia. I really do believe that our commitment to and care for people with dementia is one of the great tasks that is set before our churches today.

At around the same time that Dr Alois Alzheimer was challenging our understanding of people who were cognitively impaired, Dr Albert Schweitzer (1910) was challenging our understanding of God's presence in the world and his will for his church:

> He comes to us as One unknown, without a name, as of old by the lakeside, He came to those who knew him not. He speaks to us the same word 'follow thou me!' and sets us to the tasks which He has to fulfil for our time. He commands. And to those who obey Him, whether they be wise or simple, He will reveal Himself in the toils, the conflict, the sufferings which they shall pass through in His fellowship, and, as an ineffable mystery, they shall learn in their own experience Who He Is . . .

PART ONE

SETTING THE SCENE

Lord,
In weakness or in strength
We bear your image.
We pray for those we love
who now live in a land of shadows,
where the light of memory is dimmed,
where the familiar lies unknown,
where the beloved become as strangers.
Hold them in your everlasting arms,
and grant to those who care
    a strength to serve
    a patience to persevere,
    a love to last,
    and a peace that passes human understanding.
Hold us in your everlasting arms,
today and for all eternity;
through Jesus Christ our Lord[1]

---

[1] Using Common Worship – Funerals; RA Horton, Church House Press
2000

Chapter 1

An Opportunity offered and a Challenge set

The changing scene

Our understanding of dementia is changing and the ways in which we respond to it are changing. The last few years have seen an enormous amount of re-thinking about dementia and many exciting and creative responses to caring for people with dementia and their families have emerged. There is still a great deal to be done however. We are in the early days, but local churches can play an important part in this changing scene. Rightly understood, what they can offer are things of great importance and value, and what they can learn – about people, about community, about the role of the church and the nature of faith can, in return, be extremely humbling. There are opportunities for working with others for creative dialogue and for authentic ministry within reach of just about every congregation and church community in the country.

To face up to the presence of dementia within our midst is to discover opportunities for service and growth that are entirely consistent with the church's distinctive mission and role within society. To ignore that challenge is to raise serious questions, not only about our understanding of what it means to be a church, but also about our understanding of what it means to be human. To ignore that challenge must raise questions about our understanding of the importance of the spiritual dimension to life and to the lives of countless people, many of whom would be included in 'these, the least of my brethren'.

> It is a lavishing of precious resources, our precious ointment
> on the handicapped, the insane, the rejected and the dying
> that most clearly reveals the love of Christ in our times.
>
> It is this gratuitous caring, this unilateral declaration of love
> which proclaims the gospel more powerfully than bishops
> and theologians . . . more than anything I have discovered
> that the world is not divided into the sick and those who care
> for them, but that we are all wounded and that we all contain
> within our hearts that love which is for the healing of the
> nations. (Cassidy 1988)

The majority of people with dementia live within the community,
in their own homes or in the homes of family members. They are
spread right across the country, in towns and cities, in villages and
remote hamlets. They are to be found in prosperous and wealthy
areas, and in economically poor and socially deprived areas, in
much the same way as our churches and religious communities
are. People with dementia and their carers are sometimes very
articulate, understanding and positive (though not necessarily all
three together), or they may have difficulties in understanding
their condition and in sharing their hopes and fears (again, not
necessarily all three together). What this means is that people
with dementia and their carers are just like everyone else, a mixed
bunch. In fact they *are* everyone else, more than that, they are *us*!
We are not speaking about people who are any different from
ourselves, and like ourselves they – or we – have a whole host of
different insights, attitudes and needs. In fact, many people
reading this book may well develop dementia in the years to come,
or may already be trying to come to terms with it.

A recent book on dementia (Cheston & Bender 1999) contained
505 references and 292 of these (58%) related to literature written
within the preceding ten years. This is a simple way of illustrating
how "dementia" has become a topical and popular area of research
and reflection in recent years. It used to be a near-forgotten area
of concern, attracting few resources and little interest. Now it is a
'growth industry', but still in its infancy as regards our

understanding and the provision of appropriate services. Things are improving; in some regions quicker than in others, but there is still a long way to go. Patterns of care are extremely variable and attitudes towards people with dementia vary enormously. Great strides have been made in recent years, but we are not there yet, and there are pockets of resistance just as often as there are examples of creative and sustaining care.

It is within this climate of developing understanding and changing attitudes that local churches are offered the opportunity to share their insights and resources, and to learn, alongside others, just what it means to be human. All around them there are people engaged in the process of trying to live creatively and hopefully within the context of a serious, often terrible, illness. This little book is intended to be a guide and an encouragement to churches as they taken up these opportunities and face up to these challenges.

How shall we sing the Lord's song in a strange land?

Way back in Old Testament times, when the Babylonians attacked Judah in 587BC, the country was invaded and the Temple was ransacked and destroyed. Many people were led away into captivity, being forced to march into exile in Babylonia. Not only was this a political disaster, it was also a religious crisis. In those days God was perceived as being a territorial God. Different countries had their own deities, and for Israel and Judah Yahweh was the God who reigned. The Babylonians had their own gods, and so when the Hebrew people were led into exile they left the land of Judah and its God and entered a foreign land with foreign gods. And so in Psalm 137 we read "By the waters of Babylon we sat down and wept; when we remembered thee O Sion . . . How shall we sing the Lord's song in a strange land?"

What we now know, with hindsight, was that this time of exile was to be a particularly important time in the development of their religious understanding. To begin with, there was the discovery that God was still accessible to them in this foreign land. God was God beyond the boundaries of Israel and Judah. An astonishing discovery and experience. As people reflected on this, so there gradually emerged a whole body of religious reflection and writing, especially what we now know as chapters 40-55 of Isaiah, chapters which contain some of the most beautiful and profound verses in the whole Bible. New patterns of worship also developed, and people discovered that they could survive in their faith without the physical presence of the Temple. It was during this period that synagogues emerged as meeting places for learning and the sharing of faith.

So from a situation of apparent disaster and despair, new insights about the nature of God emerged and new experiences of God's presence and continuing care and love became clear to them.

I want to suggest that our experiences of dementia may not perhaps, be all that dissimilar. For the person with dementia and for their families and carers there is a breaking down of what has been known and trusted and accepted over the years. A future is emerging which can be very frightening. A diagnosis of dementia can be experienced as an invasion of all that has been held dear, a breaking down of, or a threat to, relationships, understanding, plans and hopes, even of Hope itself. It is very often an experience of devastation, sometimes coming very quickly, or sometimes, for other people, coming quite gradually – but still coming, whether slowly or quickly. It is a strange land which is beckoning, and will it be possible to sing the Lord's song within it? The answer that question must be – Yes, it will be possible, for many people for much of the time; the challenge is to help enable that to be the case. A further challenge is then to enable it to be possible for all people for most, or all of the time.

It is also a 'foreign land' for most churches and congregations, as we seek ways to remain in contact with people with dementia and their families and as we seek to offer support and encouragement to people whom perhaps we have never met before. It is also a new experience for many of us to work out just what is 'the Lord's song' for people who have little or no connection with our churches. The early church struggled hard to reach the understanding that a person did not first have to become a Jew before they could become a Christian. Many of our churches may have to face a similar struggle before they reach an understanding that a person does not first have to become a Christian before they can sing the Lord's song. It is surely possible to share and celebrate the most important and significant parts of our lives without necessarily speaking the same language. This is a subject we shall return to in a later chapter.

Acknowledging and facing up to our own vulnerability

Whether we are a GP, a psychiatrist, a nurse, a psychogeriatrician, a bishop, a professor or some combination of them all, or none of them, we all feel vulnerable when confronted by dementia. No-one is such an expert as not to feel very small and inadequate when seeking to understand what is happening when a person has dementia. Of course it is much worse for the person who has the illness, but also for those who seek to help and support, to encourage and stand-alongside, there is an enormous sense of inadequacy. We are confronted not only by the vulnerability of the person with dementia but also by our own vulnerability.

Vulnerability is not the same as incompetence, and we can all seek to increase our understanding, our skills and our competence, whilst acknowledging the reality of our vulnerability. Local churches and local ministry teams will also experience this sense of inadequacy and vulnerability. It is inevitable and, if the truth be told, it is probably essential if we are to engage in this work with a sense of humility and vocation. It is at these times that our most creative and authentic work probably begins, not stops. Monica Furlong (Furlong 1974) encapsulates this in her poem:

Show me not, Lord, your rich men
With their proud boasts of poverty and celibacy
They are too much for me.
Hide me from those who want to help
And still have the strength to do so.
Only those who get on with their lives
And think they have nothing to give
Are any use to me.
Let your bankrupts feed me.

So local ministry can begin where you are and with the resources that you have. If you wait until you feel you have the necessary skills and confidence, then perhaps you will never begin. But recognising your vulnerability should encourage an approach which is humble, eager to learn from others and needing to share insights and experiences. When we admit that we don't know then perhaps we are more open to hearing and seeing and to being taken by surprise. Surprise is certainly one aspect of dementia care.

Being alongside is an important ministry. Watching and waiting, and having a supportive role. These are key elements in many types of ministry, and they have a good pedigree, for the first disciples were asked to watch and pray as Jesus entered into his own particular agony in the garden. Perhaps our churches today are being asked to share in a similar ministry. Watching and waiting, being alongside, keeping awake and praying. This was not an easy task then and it is not an easy task now, but it is something which perhaps the church is being asked to do as our understanding of dementia and our desire to find appropriate forms of support and encouragement grow.

A new model is emerging

One reason why this is an exciting time for the churches to be involved in this work is because a new model of care and understanding is unfolding. Like many such changes, it comes in different places and at different speeds, but it is now possible to discern a definite shift in society's understanding of and attitudes towards dementia and dementia care. Put at its simplest this is a shift from what is often called the bio-medical (or organic) model to what is increasing being called the person-centred approach. It is dangerous to over-simplify complex things and I clearly run that risk in trying spell out, in simple terms, just what the differences between these two approaches are. They are not all one or all the other, there are vast grey areas and quite clearly we cannot say that all the 'goodies' are in one camp and the other camp has all the 'baddies', although there is often a suggestion of this in some of the literature. We must therefore be careful to recognise the insights that each model has to offer. We clearly need a fusion of the best of both, but for the sake of simplicity it is easy to set them out as contrasting and sometimes conflicting.

The bio-medical approach focuses upon the disease, whilst the person-centred approach focuses upon the person. It is sometimes expressed as

The *person with DEMENTIA*

rather than

The *PERSON with dementia.*

It is a seemingly small difference with considerable repercussions.

The bio-medical approach tends to suggest that the "person" is gradually disintegrating, until, at the end there is no person left (Fontana & Smith 1989)[2]. The person-centred approach tends to suggest that, despite the illness, the "person" remains, even though, as the illness progresses it may be more and more difficult to 'access' or communicate with that person.

The bio-medical approach has a tendency to focus upon what a person can no longer do, it can measure and chart the gradual decline in a person's capacity to do and achieve various tasks. The person-centred approach, on the other hand, tends to stress what a person is still able to do and achieve. It focuses on what skills a person still retains rather than upon what skills they have lost.

The bio-medical approach has a tendency to 'look beyond' the person with dementia and discuss their diagnosis, symptoms or treatment with their family or carers. The person-centred approach would perhaps be more willing to involve the person with dementia as much as possible in all discussions and decisions about their situation.

At those times when there may be some form of challenging or anti-social behaviour, the bio-medical model would be primarily concerned with *managing and controlling* the behaviour, the person-centred approach would lay a greater emphasis upon trying to *understand* what lies behind such behaviour.

The bio-medical model tends to see dementia as a disease and the person-centred approach tends to see it as a disability.

---

[2] This article gives us one of the 'classic' examples of the biomedical approach: "the self has slowly unravelled and 'unbecome' a self, but the caregivers . . . assume that there is a person behind the largely unwitting presentation of self of the victims, albeit in reality there is less and less, until where once there was a unique individual there is but emptiness".

The bio-medical model has tended to pay little heed to the experiences of the person with dementia whilst the person-centred approach seeks to elicit and engage with what the person with dementia experiences and feels.

"In the eyes of the clinician, the person becomes 'a patient' with cognitive and neurological problems, who is socially incompetent and in need of medication, constant risk assessment, containment in safe environments, and protection from accidents. The views of the individual person and meaningful patient-doctor interactions are gradually lost to care plans. This is not to say that the clinicians are doing a bad job; they are simply doing the job they were taught to do – methodically and with much integrity." (Lawrence 2003)

This list could be extended, but these few examples serve to illustrate the nature of the shift in thinking. I am conscious of portraying the bio-medical model as almost entirely negative, and of course this is clearly not the case, but I have made that emphasis in order to highlight areas in which a different understanding is being offered by the advocates of a person-centred approach.

The effects of a pattern of care which is primarily bio-medical is movingly described by Sharon Waller (Waller 2002):

In the last year of my father's life he became a man with Alzheimer's. Although he was called by his name, he was defined by his dementia. He was in the culture of a subset consisting of the oldest-old, the dependent, the infirm and the senile. Sometimes it seemed that people regarded his dementia as the most important piece of information about him. The condition of Alzheimer's was used as identification, as a reason, and as a predictor. At times, this information was used to hastily decide what he could and couldn't do, understand and feel. It provided reason enough to speak and act in a certain way and not another. It defined the quality of many of his interactions. My father's dementia was at least as much socially and culturally constructed as it was medically defined.

This daughter's view of dementia, which can be said to encompass the new approach can be contrasted with a son's view which is still rooted in the older approach – they are not writing about the same person, by the way:

> It's got him and it's slowly, capriciously losing him, rubbing him out so that in the end, all that will be left is the whine of dementia and a hieroglyph that looks like him" (Gill 2003)

The reason for spelling out this contrasting approach to dementia care so clearly this early in the book is because it is highly likely that congregations have several (if not many) people in their midst who are committed to the older approach. They often view the new understandings – if they have ever actually come across them – with considerable scepticism, even with hostility in some cases. I have met many doctors, nurses and care-workers within our churches who still maintain a fixed and inflexible attitude towards people with dementia which almost screams out for the insights of person-centred care.

One of the leading voices in the shift towards a new understanding of and attitude towards dementia was that of Tom Kitwood, who described the scene in this way (Kitwood 1997):

> Around 1980 the prevailing view of the conditions known as 'primary degenerative dementia' was that they presented a hopeless picture. Care for those who were affected was seen mainly as a matter of giving attention to basic physical needs while the process of degeneration in nerve tissue took its inexorable course. Generally it was believed that very little could be done in a truly therapeutic way through direct human intervention. No radical changes would be brought about until medical science had elucidated the underlying biochemistry and emerged with treatments that would arrest

or prevent the pathological process. In effect, the *person* with dementia did not exist; 'going senile' was a sentence to radical exclusion.

Now, however, the whole situation looks very different . ...

The churches, in our patterns of ministry, have a long tradition of this "new" type of approach and care, which is theoretically there even if not always present in practice. We come from a tradition of hope, of affirmation and of the centrality and abiding nature of individual worth, and so we ought to be able to embrace this new culture of dementia care and in so doing help promote its spread. The situation offers us wonderful opportunities for caring and serving, for learning and sharing, but such opportunities also present us with formidable challenges.

Lord, in a bewildering world full of confusing images and conflicting sounds
    you have surrounded your church with men and women
    whose work and insight can inspire and sustain.
Grant it the grace and humility to learn from them with
    gratitude.
Grant it also, the eyes and ears of compassion,
    to discern opportunities for service,
    and a heart strengthened by steadfast courage
    to accept the challenges involved.

In a Strange Land...

PART TWO

TOWARDS AN UNDERSTANDING OF CARE FOR PEOPLE WITH DEMENTIA

Dementia care is a very dynamic field to be in at present. This has not always been the case. Until ten or so years ago it was characterised by profound therapeutic nihilism. The combination of characteristics: old age, challenging behaviour, incompetence, loss of insight, low status, increasing numbers and poor success in pharmacological research cast a deep shadow. Much of dementia care still operates in this shadow, but a much more optimistic and dynamic approach is becoming the norm.[3]

Professor Mary Marshall, C.B.E.
Director of the Dementia Services Development Centre
The University of Stirling

---

[3] From the Introduction to *State of the art in dementia care* Centre for Policy on Ageing 1997

Chapter 2

Getting our Heads around Dementia

Definitions

The words *senile dementia* are seldom used now. 'Senility' conjures up a negative image and there are many positives to be found within the world of dementia care. Similarly, the term *pre-senile dementia* has now been replaced by the more accurate description *early onset dementia.* There is also a growing use of the phrase *people (or person) with dementia* rather than the objectionable *demented* which so easily strips a person of their humanity or *dementia sufferers* which focuses upon the illness and its negative experience rather than upon the person. These are small things in themselves, but indicative of a radical change in understanding and approach. Few people in our churches are likely to be experts in understanding dementia, but we can all endeavour to become expert in honouring and affirming people with dementia. The ways in which we view them and speak about them are essential parts of that process.

The word *Dementia* is an umbrella term, it is used to describe or hold together a range of different and specific illnesses. As a Latin word it simply means 'out of one's mind' and it is usually used when three types of symptoms are present in a single person. When there is an impairment in their short-term memory, when there are problems in another area of cognition (such as language) and when there are problems in daily social living.

Rather like the word 'weather' is used to hold together winter and summer, rain and sunshine, hot and cold, hurricane or tornado, so when we are told that someone 'has dementia' our thinking is directed along a certain path, but we have to ascertain just what type of dementia the person has. Just as to say that a person is a 'scientist' does not tell us a great deal until we know whether he or she is a mathematician, a geologist, a biochemist or an astro-physicist.

We use the word *Dementia* to cover a collection of symptoms that may be caused by a number of different illnesses. They relate to the progressive failure of functions of the brain and to its continuing physical deterioration. We do not yet fully know what causes these illnesses, nor do we have any cure for them. Research is progressing in both of these areas, but no adequate answers have yet been found to the questions. Drugs have evolved which may slow down the progression of the illness for some people, in some circumstances. We shall return to a discussion about drugs later on.

The most common forms of dementia are:

- Alzheimer's disease - often referred to as DAT
- Vascular dementia - also called multi-infarct dementia (MID) or arteriosclerotic dementia
- Lewy body disease (LBD)
- Frontal temporal dementia
- Korsakoff's disease
- Pick's disease
- Creutzfeldt-Jakob disease (CJD), and
- AIDS related dementia
- Dementia related to Huntingdon's and Parkinson's diseases

There are others too, but these are the most common ones. The most usual type of dementia is Alzheimer's disease, with approximately 60% of all cases, followed by vascular dementia which accounts for 25-30%. Some people have both Alzheimer's and vascular dementia. One expert (Jacques 1992) has tentatively suggested that for every 60 cases of Alzheimer's disease there are 20 cases of vascular dementia and 20 cases where the person has both.

What is happening to the brain?

There are now several books which attempt to describe what is happening to the brain in a way which is relatively accessible to the person without medical knowledge. Alan Jacques's *Understanding Dementia*, mentioned above, is one of the best. A different approach is taken by the engaging story of David Snowdon's work in studying a community of nuns and his scientific work in noting their ageing process and the incidence of Alzheimer's disease (Snowdon 2001). This important piece of research is written up in a way that reads almost like a novel.

Different types of dementia affect the brain in different ways, but this is usually only detectable by sophisticated scanning techniques or by dissection of the brain during a post-mortem. The different ways in which the brain is affected generally produce the same or similar types of symptoms, which makes diagnosis a difficult procedure. There are certain complex clues, which some highly trained people may be able to detect, but for most people, their experience of observing people with dementia suggests that it is extremely difficult to differentiate one type from another. For this reason, I shall tend to use the generic word 'dementia' when discussing issues that may be related to the different specific illnesses, or to a combination of them. Jane Crisp adopted a similar approach in her excellent book for carers *Keeping in Touch with someone who has Alzheimer's* (Crisp 2000)

Most people, in my experience, seem to want a simpler explanation of what is going on in the brain than the majority of books can offer. The scenario I sketch out here must be understood as giving the broadest of pictures. In no way should it be taken as a factually accurate description – but, for all that, I think it helps us to see the general pattern, the big picture. It endeavours to explain complex biological processes in a simple picture language.

I am going to describe three things that happen within the brain when a person suffers from dementia. It is important to recognise that the brain is but one part, albeit an important part, of a person. The person who has dementia, who has some form of breakdown within their brain, is still a person and we should never forget that. A person who loses a limb, is still a person. So is someone with heart problems, so is someone with cancer – and so are those who have a particular deteriorating process within their brain. Always remember that we are *relating* to a *person* with dementia, not *responding* to a *medical problem* that happens to be located within a human frame.

Our brain weighs approximately two to two and a half pounds and is about the size of a smallish Christmas pudding. When trying to describe the effect of Alzheimer's disease I like to suggest that we think of the brain as looking rather like a sponge. As the disease develops, so the small holes in the sponge grow bigger and at the same time the whole sponge begins to shrink a little. In much the same way, the brain reduces in size and gaps appear. Snowdon, using a slightly different image, describes it in this way

> The intricate, tightly packed ruts and grooves of the cerebral cortex, which forms the surface of the brain, are also changed. Now they appear as pronounced mountains and valleys, with gaping spaces between them. (Snowdon 2001).

A second process going on in the brain relates to the development of tiny, microscopic plaques and tangles. The image which comes to mind when thinking about plaques is rust, and I suggest that we imagine that, in many different parts of the brain there is some evidence of infinitely small pieces of rust or tarnish. Of course, the substance that makes up our brains cannot rust, but if it were metal, then probably rusting would be a helpful analogy. The way I make sense of tangles is by thinking about a woollen garment which, as it gets worn often develops lots of tiny hairs which tend to take the edge off the garment. Similarly with the brain, some people develop incredibly microscopically small tiny hairs, tails or tangles at the end of the neurones in their brain.

The third image which I find helpful is to imagine that the brain is composed of thousands of millions of little transmitters and receivers, all communicating and giving evidence of a hive of activity. It is a little like moving the dial on our radio and hearing dozens of different programmes, some of which we understand and many of which we do not. When a person has dementia, particularly vascular dementia, these transmitters and receivers are slowly zapped out in an apparently random sort of way. It can have been going on for years without anyone knowing. Occasionally an 'important' transmitter or receiver is affected and we may lose access to an important part of our being. Perhaps relating to our modesty, or to our ability to observe social conventions, or, very often to the way that we access parts of our memory. Sometimes a 'crucial' transmitter or receiver is affected and we may lose our mobility or our speech and we say that we have had a 'stroke'. Vascular dementia can be over-simplified and described as a process of thousands of minute strokes apparently randomly affecting the brain.

For our purposes it is not necessary for us to understand the technicalities of what is happening to the brain. The important thing is that we know and accept that the person with dementia has an illness, a disability[4], the roots of which we cannot see. At times this will mean that we need to be more accepting, less hasty, more vigilant and less dismissive. As we shall explore later, very often

---

[4] See chapter 4 *The Limitations of the Organic Model* in Cheston & Bender's *Understanding Dementia* for a discussion about how we need to take on board the idea of dementia as a disability rather than a disease. Kitwood (1997b) says "Alzheimer's does not meet the criterion of classical disease, that distinct pathological features should be present in all cases where the symptoms appear and in none of the cases where they do not".

in our relationships with people with dementia it is *we* who are the problem rather than they.

Grasping a wider perspective

My introduction to the work of Tom Kitwood was more than a little daunting when I was confronted by an apparent mathematical equation.

$$D = B + P + NI + H + SP$$

to which I would now like to add the letter E. But in those 8 (now 9) letters there lies the foundation for a whole new understanding of and approach to dementia.

We need to unpack the letters to see what Kitwood was getting at:

Dementia is equal to, or must be understood as, the sum total of a person's **B**iography or life history, their **P**ersonality, their **N**eurological **I**mpairment (or specific illness), their general **H**ealth and the whole web of relationships that surrounds them – their **S**ocial **P**sychology. And to this list I would want to add their **E**thnicity.

It has been suggested more recently (Moore 2003) that yet another factor should be added to the equation, that of PSE - the person's **P**hysical **S**ensory **E**nvironment. Virginia Moore argues that people's behaviour is influenced greatly by their environment and that they tend to react in ways which they think are appropriate to that environment. An environment which lacks stimulation can lead to a person being withdrawn, whilst one which is too stimulating can over-activate the person with dementia.

So the equation now reads

Dementia = a person's life history + their personality + their specific illness + their general health + their network of relationships + their ethnic identity + their physical sensory environment.

Each of these variables complements and helps interpret the others. If we wish to understand better the person with dementia and if we are seeking to be alongside that person in the role of minister then it is essential that we try to reach this overall picture, this wider perspective. We shall return to the implications of this later.

Age and sex profiles

It is often claimed that dementia is an inevitable part of the process of growing old. It is not, although it is true that the incidence of dementia increases with age. Even so, when people are in their nineties it is still a minority of people, about a third, who have dementia. The figures below (Goldsmith 1996) give an approximate indication of a person's likelihood of having dementia as their age increases.

Age group (years)	% Likelihood of having dementia	% Likelihood of *not* having dementia
60-64	0.7	99.3
65-69	1.4	98.6
70-74	2.8	97.2
75-79	5.6	94.4
80-84	10.5	89.5
85-90	20.8	79.2
90-95	38.6	61.4

Figures like these should be treated with caution, and they may underestimate the number of people in the early stages of dementia, where diagnosis is extremely difficult. Nevertheless, the overall picture is that even when people reach their nineties, there is a two to one chance that they will not develop dementia. Interestingly, Snowdon (2001) suggests that the incidence of

Alzheimer's increases with age, hits a plateau at about 95 and then declines.

Another way of looking at the figures, again to be treated with caution, is to say that –

- if Britain has a population of some 55 million, then
- 9 million will be over 65, and
- there will possibly be 500,000 to 600,000 people with dementia, of whom
  - o   15,000 to 20,000 will be under 45 years of age
  - o   200,000 to 300,000 will be under 80 years of age, and
  - o   300,000 plus will be aged 80 and over

Even with such crude figures as these, it should be possible to make a very rough estimate of the number of people in any church congregation or on any church roll who may possibly have dementia. If you are unable to come up with any approximate figure then it may be because your community is failing to engage with a true cross section of society, or it may be because you have not yet begun to realise just how prevalent this condition is. I write this not to shame members of local churches but to encourage them, and I write it as a person who ministered to one congregation for six years without even being aware of the nature of dementia let alone being alert to those who may have had it!

It was thought until very recently that men were just as likely to develop dementia as women. Research now suggests that there is a greater risk for women, added to which, because there are more elderly women than elderly men, there are overall, more women with dementia than men. Also, again because of the demographic structure of our society, most of the elderly women will be either single or widowed, whilst most, though not all, of the men with dementia will have a living wife. This could well present specific pastoral implications, and will be looked at more closely later. There are also indications now that, the higher the level of education a person has, the less is the likelihood of them getting dementia.[5]

Although most people with dementia are elderly, and the older you get the greater is your likelihood of getting dementia, it has to be stressed that dementia is not an illness for the elderly alone. As the figures above indicate there may be in the region of 20,000 people in Britain under the age of 45 who have been diagnosed with the condition. The onset of dementia for someone who is still at work and who possibly has considerable commitments in terms of a spouse and family, caring for parents and repaying a mortgage brings its own sense of devastation. It has been suggested (Whalley 1997) that at 40 years of age less than one person in a thousand will have been admitted to hospital with dementia and perhaps three or four times that number will be suffering from some form of cognitive impairment:

> Coming to terms with a terminal disease at any age requires an investment of mental and emotional energy. An unexpected diagnosis of dementia at a young age complicates the process of acceptance, because thought-processing and coping mechanisms are themselves affected by the illness. (Walton 1999)

Where do people live?

Most people with dementia live within the community, with only about 6% living in some type of institutional setting. Of those living within the community who are aged 85 and over, about 25% of men live alone and about 50% of women live alone. But, as we have already noted, as there are far more elderly women than men, the number who live alone is far more than twice the actual number of men. Of those who do not live alone, most will live with their partner, siblings or children. As we shall discuss later,

---

[5] The research referred to in this paragraph is discussed more fully in chapter 7 of Cheston & Bender's *Understanding Dementia*.

there is a specific ministry needed to these family members as well as, and in addition to the ministry to the person with dementia. The Alzheimer's Society for Great Britain (AS-GB 2000) has estimated that about one third of people with dementia live alone and it is predicted (AS-GB 1994) that this figure will have almost doubled by 2011 to reach an estimated 245,000.

Because dementia is a progressive illness, people may well move from one type of accommodation to another. Perhaps living alone or with a partner to begin with, moving in with their children (or their children moving in with them) as their condition deteriorates, and then perhaps moving into some form of residential accommodation such as a nursing home – which may or may not have dementia specific accommodation - or hospital. Such moves will invariably be surrounded by considerable stress and often (though not always) with a profound sense of loss and grief, both for the person with dementia and also for their primary carers.

Recent years have seen a growing concern about the differences in, and opportunities for, care packages for people with dementia who live in rural areas (Innes 2003). There are fewer services available, there are the problems associated with travel and there is a likelihood that family members are more dispersed. Wenger argued (Wenger 2001) that there are a number of myths surrounding older people living in rural communities, such as :–

- that they have strong family support networks
- that they belong to an integrated community
- that they have better health, and that
- that they live in pleasanter surroundings which means that they will make a lower demand on services.

There is no evidence to suggest that these assumptions are true, hence Wenger's use of the term 'myth'. It is likely, therefore, that there are more obvious and specific forms of ministry open to the churches in rural areas.

Back to the beginning

Richard Cheston and Michael Bender begin their book *Understanding Dementia – the Man with Worried Eyes* in a highly graphic and arresting way:

> April 1906: On the Munich train drawing out of Frankfurt station is a man in the uniform of an employee of the Municipal Mental Asylum. He guards carefully a large container. We cannot see inside it, but he knows it protects a large jar, and in that jar, bathed in preserving fluid, is a brain, the brain of Frau Auguste D, who was admitted into the asylum on 25 November 1901. The admitting doctor who clerked her in was the senior physician, Dr Alois Alzheimer, who recorded her severely disturbed and disorientated behaviour.
>
> Dr Alzheimer left Frankfurt in 1903 but, always interested in brain structures, had an agreement that when Frau Auguste D died her brain would be sent to him. By 1906 he was working in the Anatomical Laboratory of the Royal Psychic Clinic, Munich. That was to be the final resting place of Frau Auguste D's brain.

We have come a long way in the past hundred years in understanding the nature of dementia and in responding to and caring for people with dementia. There is still a long way to go. Dementia care is still in its infancy. Local churches and congregations have the opportunity to share in this important work.

For I am persuaded that neither height nor depth – nor
   anything else in the whole of creation, is able to separate
   us from the love of God.
So help me Lord, when the confusions and contradictions of
   dementia seem to threaten that persuasion;
   when the glorious intricacies of our brains seem to
   develop minds and directions of their own.
Strengthen our belief that each person is precious in your
   sight, no matter how strong or weak, healthy or sick,
   remembering or forgetful.
For nothing can separate us from your love

Chapter 3

Some Conditions relating to Dementia

So, when all this activity and change is taking place within the brain, what is happening to the person, how is their behaviour and their mood affected, what are the consequences of having such an illness? We must always remember that people are unique individuals and therefore refrain from making blanket assertions, because the illnesses develop a particular path specific to each individual, and no two people's dementia is the same. There are, however, a number if variables which are often to be found associated with the illnesses. Few people will manifest all of them, but most people will show some of them, and they become the distinctive traits by which people begin to recognise what we mean by the word 'dementia'.

Memory

'Having problems with my memory' is one of the first intimations of dementia. But this does not mean that everyone who has memory problems has dementia – and that is an important truth to stress right at the beginning. There are many reasons why people's memory may be affected. It could be the after-effects of an anaesthetic, it could be related to particular drugs that a person is taking, it could be related to depression or to a poor diet; all these things will need to be explored by the person's GP. However, if a person has dementia then at some stage, definitely and progressively, their memory will deteriorate.

To begin with, it is the short-term memory which is affected. People forget information which they have just been given, they forget where they have placed something or why they were going into a particular room or to see a certain person. They may be in the middle of cooking a meal when they are distracted by something – the door bell or the telephone, and then they forget what they were doing before the interruption. They forget messages they were supposed to hand on to someone, and they may begin to forget the subject of the conversation that they are engaged in. They may forget whether they have told you something, and repeat it, perhaps several times. The brain is failing to store appropriate information in the appropriate way. Events of today and yesterday may be confused or forgotten, but events of twenty, forty or sixty years ago may be as clear as a bell. Information received and filed away when the brain was unaffected by the illness is still accessible, but that which is more recent becomes more and more inaccessible. A friend of mine enjoys listening to tapes of radio comedy programmes whilst travelling. He admits that his wife finds this very trying as she has heard them so many times before, but, because he cannot remember them, each time he hears a joke he bursts into laughter – it is as though he was hearing it for the first time. He is aware of this and says it is one of the benefits of his illness – he is constantly being amused by his stock of audio tapes!

Problems with memory will continue. People may begin to forget where they parked their car, how to get out of the car-park (McGowin 1993) or how to find their way home. They may begin to forget how to use household equipment – the video, the telephone, the cooker or the kettle. They may then begin to forget the names of things – fork, table, or toilet for instance. All this takes place over a longish period of time, of course, perhaps over three to eight years – it is difficult to place any precise timing, people are so very different.

People may forget names, and then may forget relationships. Daughters are mistaken as mothers, sons as brothers, friends as relatives and relatives as work colleagues. At this stage, the person with dementia may be registering that they know that the person is significant to them, but they are unable to place them in the appropriate context, whether it be of time or place or relationship. To mistake a son and think that he is a person's father may be distressing for the son but also, strangely enough, quite flattering, because the person knows that this is someone to whom they are closely attached in a familial relationship. A friend who nursed his wife through to her death once asked her if she knew who he was; she looked at him, smiled and said "No, but you are very, very nice". He was delighted.

There is an ongoing discussion in dementia care as to whether a person has *lost their memory* or whether they have *lost access to their memory*. This is because it is not uncommon for a person with dementia to have occasional very lucid moments when they seem able to recall events and people that had apparently been lost forever. Such moments may only last a very short while, but they are quite remarkable.

Another experience which may cause surprise is when a person who has almost ceased to speak in any way that we can at the moment make any sense of, begins to sing and may well sing several verses of a popular song or of a hymn with near-perfect enunciation. I recall visiting a lady when she was quite close to death, I had been to see her several times after I learned of her existence in a local nursing home. I did not find them easy visits; she was curled up on her bed, moaning and twisting around and showing virtually no signs of knowing that I was present. After a short while I said a prayer and was amazed to hear the word "Amen" when I finished. I left her room feeling very inadequate and yet deeply moved by the experience.

Wandering

Wandering is regarded by many of the people who care for people with dementia as being one of the most troubling and difficult things that they have to come to terms with (Cantes & Rigby 1997). It has been described as "a collective term for a complex of behavioural presentations for which there is no magical cure" (Lai & Arthur 2003).

Kate Allen observed that:

> It is one of the most challenging behavioural problems in dementia, making demands upon the coping skills even of those with extensive training and experience in the field. When people who wander have to be cared for in settings which are not geared to dealing with the behaviour and the problems it can cause, the resulting strain and anxiety can be enormous . . . wandering is a complex and challenging behaviour demanding an individualised and imaginative approach. Although there are no straightforward solutions, careful observation and thoughtful interventions can reduce wandering, or remove the need for it. (Allen 1994)

Wandering can take several forms; from going for extended walks in the locality to pacing up and down in the confines of a bedroom. Sometimes it may seem quite purposeful and at other times appear to be totally meaningless and compulsive. It presents carers with a two-fold challenge: how to understand or interpret it, and secondly, how to manage or control it so that the person does not endanger themselves or others.

In the early stages of the illness the person with dementia may want to go out walking, and may walk for several hours a day, covering mile after mile. Problems arise when they forget where they have come from and begin to get lost. One way of addressing this problem is to ensure that the person carries a card giving their name and address – such cards are often available from local branches of the Alzheimer's Society. A time may come, of course, when the person forgets that they carry such a card, and I have known people pin a discrete label on the person's lapel. Sometimes, when people are distressed at being lost they can receive sympathetic help from people whom they meet, but at other times they may be shunned because people think that they are drunk or behaving unusually. When people wander for a couple of hours or so this can bring a little respite for their carers at home, but usually, and increasingly the carers become concerned because they don't know where the person is and they don't know if they are safe. Problems increase as the illness progresses. The person may begin to do dangerous things like walking in the middle of the road, visiting a park and going on the swings, trying to climb a tree or walk into other people's gardens and homes.

Another problem is that the person may become unaware of the time of day and choose to go out walking at eleven o'clock at night or four o'clock in the morning. Or they may go out inappropriately dressed; wearing a summer dress in the middle of winter, a heavy overcoat and gloves in the middle of a heatwave, or quite commonly, going out in their night-clothes in the middle of the day.

Wandering can also take place within the home. Some people with dementia seem to need to be always on the move, going from room to room or walking round and round in the same room. Some types of residential care buildings have been especially designed to enable people to wander, so that they can walk along the corridors even, in some establishments, doing a figure of eight circuit.

But why do people seem to want to wander? McGregor and Bell (1994) are convinced that:

> Genuine 'aimless' wandering only occurs when people are sedated. People with dementia rarely set off without a purpose, they are always anxious to go somewhere specific, for their own good reasons. For instance, they may believe that they must get home to prepare tea for their children returning from school, or that they need to look after their parents who are ill . . .

So, it is increasingly being thought now that people with dementia have their own reasons for wanting to wander, that it is not an involuntary activity triggered by some activity in the brain. The challenge is for us to discover what it is that is prompting the wandering:

> What carers need is the capacity to be able to cope with the behaviour, and then the skill to be able to interpret the reason behind it, and the ability to respond in such a way as to reassure the person and calm their anxieties – not by distracting them but by resolving what inner conflict sparked off the behaviour in the first place. (Goldsmith 1996)

In terms of ministry there is much-needed support that can be offered to family carers, especially if we are willing and able to sit alongside the person with dementia and help in the process of trying to discover just what it is that he or she is trying to communicate by such activity.

Challenging behaviour

Someone asked me if the term 'challenging behaviour' meant the ways in which we challenge the sometimes anti-social behaviour of people with dementia. That is precisely what it is not! The term is used to describe those forms of behaviour which are a real challenge for us to understand and cope with. Some people with dementia, in the later stages, can occasionally turn violent and strike out at people who are near to them. Another form of challenging behaviour is when the person cries out, shouts, screams and seems unwilling and/or unable to be pacified. These types of behaviour often have nothing whatsoever to do with how the person was before they became ill. So a sweet-tempered person may break out into fits of anger, a quiet and loveable person may strike out or throw things at their husband, wife or visitor. Someone who has never uttered a swear word in their life may come out with the most foul and abusive language. Some people may become quite destructive with furniture or possessions, or may daub the bathroom walls with excreta. However the challenging behaviour manifests itself it can be distressing for the people around them, and often acutely embarrassing. It can also be extremely taxing, wearisome or annoying. But what is it like for the person with dementia?

Trying to understand and cope with aggression or other forms of challenging behaviour can sometimes be helped by setting the behaviour in the context of a number of questions.

- What is the nature of the challenging behaviour?
- To whom, particularly, is it a problem?
- How often does behaviour of this kind occur?
- How long does it continue for?
- Who is at risk (the person with dementia? other people?)
- How can any risks be minimised?
- Can we determine what were the causes of the behaviour – what triggered it off?

Martin Luther King once said that "violence was the voice of the unheard", and an increasing number of people involved in dementia care are of the view that the person with dementia is actually trying to communicate something by their behaviour. How can you communicate when your words fail? When you cannot formulate what you want to say? When the harder you try the more difficult things seem to be?

There are now countless examples of people beginning to understand what lies behind such behaviour and therefore being in a position to address the situation more appropriately.

- One woman was proving to be more than the staff could cope with in a nursing home; it was only when it was discovered that she was suffering from toothache but couldn't communicate this to anyone that the problem was resolved.

- Another man, who used to react quite violently if he was ever startled turned out to have had a distinguished military career in situations of intense danger.

- A man who was seen to be a problem early each morning was later understood to have been a shepherd in the Highlands of Scotland and he needed to be off early each morning to tend his flock. The attempts at restraint by the staff invariably led to outbursts of violence until this was understood; it was accepted that his whole life had been based upon getting up early and about his business, and therefore he could not fit into the nursing home regime very easily. They found ways of engaging the man in early morning routines, 'before the day started'.

Once the problem has been identified, then good dementia care finds ways of reacting appropriately.

Another way in which behavioural problems are approached is by using the **ABC** technique. This asks a number of questions about the

             Antecedents, the

             Behaviour and the

             Consequences.

Again the emphasis is upon *understanding* the behaviour rather than attempting to *control* it. This is sometimes quite difficult for carers, who may be at their wits end, and what they often want is some form of drug intervention, "what Michele and I are after is a chemical solution" (Grant 1998). As Jackson & MacDonald (2003) point out, "Football hooligans are not sedated in anticipation of the possibility that they *might* harm others. Is it right to do so in dementia care?"

Modern dementia care tends to believe that there is always an explanation for aggressive outbursts or verbal abuse. The difficulty is in discovering just what that explanation is. It might arise from

- misunderstanding personal care and experiencing it as an intrusion or invasion of their privacy, especially if it is being done by a person of the opposite sex

- having some insight into the nature of their condition and trying to hide it from others and cope with it by themselves, and in this process probably feeling both frustrated and frightened

- the sheer exasperation of being unable to do a particular task

- finding it difficult to cope with a social or physical situation and feeling threatened by it

- feeling that the person caring for them at that moment is being unsympathetic or confusing

- not having sufficient stimulation, either in terms of activity or conversation or engagement

- being too hot or too cold, or the room being draughty or lacking in air

- being over-tired

- feeling that their remaining skills are being overlooked and therefore that they are being made to feel even more dependent

- experiencing a lack of consistency in their care, with too many different people being involved at different times of the day

- feeling that they are physically restrained, perhaps not being able to get out of their chair, or leave the room or go outside

- having inappropriate medication.

There are clearly many reasons why a person may engage in challenging behaviour, and it is important that we try to understand what lies behind such behaviour. It is not helpful to scold the person, to blame them or seek to punish them in some way or other. This behaviour is the cry of a deeply distressed and hurting person, the challenge is, how are we to understand their situation and respond and react accordingly. It is not an easy thing to do.

Maureen Russell (2001), in a fascinating article, reflected theologically on her experience of caring for her husband's Aunt Mae, who was 88 years old and had dementia:

> As in all relationships, there are issues of power and authority. Because of dementia, Mae's world is cognitively different from mine. The loss of some of her mental powers, however, does not mean that she does not have a sense of her own identity. She has feelings about herself – her dignity, and pride need to be treated with respect which should never be denied or undermined. Moreover, because she asserts herself when she can, she is compelling others to rethink their attitudes by challenging those who would seek to diminish her. Her anger, frustration and pain are signs of such a challenge. It is evident too, that she feels a sense of well-being and contentment when she is treated with sensitivity and consideration.

> No truly fulfilling relationships are one-sided. On the face of it, those looking after people with dementia are often viewed as being heroic. Certainly, such caring is not easy and the trauma of dementia's manifestations needs to be faced realistically. One must not, however, sink into a mode of self-sacrificing slavery, nor feel compelled to behave like a saint to keep control. I find it helpful at times of stress to remember that the relationship between Mae and myself is mutual and not suzerain. She has ways of exerting influence and power too. While, on the one hand Mae cannot help herself, there are occasions when she uses, quite strategically

as a weapon, that which does come under her control, for example her bodily functions.

Depression

There is a close and complex relationship between dementia and depression and they often display the same or similar symptoms. So much so that there is a condition known as pseudo-dementia which is when the person gives every indication of having dementia but is, in fact, suffering from depression. A person who is extremely depressed may appear to have dementia and a person who has dementia is often extremely depressed. This is one reason why it is often very difficult for doctors to arrive at a correct diagnosis of dementia.

People with dementia often become apathetic, showing a lack of initiative and this, coupled with the growing loss of skills may lead to further withdrawal from daily activities. Such a withdrawal from pleasurable, meaningful and relational activities can then result in a depressed mood with further withdrawal and a consequent deepening depression (Lewinsohn et al 1991). Whilst there are only a few drugs which can address the issues of Alzheimer's disease, there is a whole range of drugs which can be used to alleviate depression. It is not uncommon to come across situations where depression is just accepted as something that has to be lived with, without much attempt being made to counteract it. Carers therefore should press hard to ensure that even though the person may have dementia the symptoms of depression are taken seriously in their own right, and addressed.

Grief

Until you open your eyes to your own predicament you cannot see the extent of it. However, if opening your eyes

means seeing . . . devastating limitations is it bearable?"
(Sinason 1992)[6]

The work of Elisabeth Kubler Ross (1970) has been enlightening
and supporting much of our ministry to the dying and the bereaved
for many years now. She spelled out various stages that people
went through in the process of grieving – denial, anger,
depression, bargaining and acceptance. There has been criticism
over the years that such an approach is too rigid, and that people
may well be in several of these stages at the same time and that
you cannot predict a clear progression from one to the other. By
and large, these criticisms have been understood and accepted.
Nevertheless, it remains true that Kubler Ross gave us a
framework and a vocabulary which have been extremely helpful in
coming to an understanding of death, dying and grieving and in
helping us cope with these situations with a certain degree of
hope, creativity and high regard.

There is a similar but not identical process of grieving taking place
when a person has dementia. The experience of a person with
dementia will be explored more fully in the next two chapters, but
it is important that at this early stage we recognise how important
it is for us to take seriously the manifold experiences of loss that
dementia entails.

Coulson (1993) identified five stages of grief resolution, based on
clinical experience, that people with dementia seem to go through:

- desperation
- disconnection
- anger
- depression, before
- images of the twilight

The person with dementia needs to find a way of looking into the
future with equanimity and trust rather than with fear and dread.

---

[6] See especially the chapter 'The man who was losing his brain'

Any help that ministers can give in this process really will be a sharing in that process of healing and wholeness which is at the heart of the gospel.

"Remember now thy creator" – if only all people could!
How do those whose hold on the past is slipping maintain a
    sense of belonging?
    The truth is that our faith depends not upon us remembering
    you but upon you remembering us.
For those who wander from the pathway,
        we rely upon the belief that there is nowhere we
        can travel to which is beyond your presence.
For all who rant and rave,
        for all who lash out at others,
        for all who step beyond our sense of what is
        acceptable,
        we ask your blessing.
For all who sink into depression,
        or who are overwhelmed by a sense of grief,
        we ask your peace.
"Remember now thy children" – how good that you do!

Chapter 4

The Experience of Dementia

This day is mine
I've yet to know tomorrow
I'll use it well
For who can tell
If joy will come or sorrow.
What was can be no more
What is can be today
I'll use the day for all it's worth
Before it too will fade away. (Helen 1994)

I'm not stupid, I'm sick . . . . . .
I have Alzheimer's , so what! I've got too many
things to do to be spending precious time worrying
about it. (Lee 2003)

People often wonder what it must be like to have dementia, and if
people who have it are aware of what is happening. It is only
within the last ten or fifteen years that much attention has been
paid to what is now called 'the subjective experience of dementia'.
Robert Davis, an American pastor, was probably the first to record
his experiences to a wide public when, in 1987, together with his
wife he published the book *My Journey into Alzheimer's Disease.*
It is a graphic and moving account and probably essential reading
for people wishing to explore Christian ministry in this field. In
many ways it is a depressing book and I like to reflect that
thinking about dementia care has developed and improved over
the intervening period. His wife, in the epilogue to the book,
writes what many people must feel the world over. But I also
believe that many people have found a more heartening and
hopeful route through this valley of distress, and we shall be
exploring such possibilities later:

Death would be better than this – to hold on to the box when the present is used up – hoping the box can bring again the joy of the reality of the gift – but the box is empty! This is what one has to look forward to with Alzheimer's disease. The body of the one you love – devoid of all expression, of recognition, of joy – here but not here. You are destined to live with the memory of who he was. How do you prepare for the holocaust? (Davis 1987)

Six years later Diana Friel McGowin a former legal assistant and freelance writer wrote about her experiences (McGowin 1993). At the time when she was writing she was clear that it was possible to re-learn some of the things that she had forgotten. She also noted that there were good days as well as bad ones. Her book is a passionate plea that we should find ways of enabling people to live with this disability by stressing what they are still able to do rather than what they can no longer do. A point of view which now underlies a great deal of good dementia care work.

Reflecting on these two books John Keady and Jane Gilliard (Keady and Gilliard 1999) note that professional interventions are hardly mentioned in them, and on the few occasions that they are, they are mentioned with feelings of frustration and hostility. Both Davis and McGowin expressed disquiet at:

- the time taken to establish a diagnosis
- the fact that they were kept in the dark about the outcomes of investigative examinations
- the lack of appropriate support services, particularly support groups to facilitate discussion
- the inadequate supply of information, and
- the lack of support for memory training.

Christine Boden was 46 years old when she was diagnosed with Alzheimer's disease and her book *Who will I be when I die?* chronicles her physical, emotional and spiritual journey in the first three years after her diagnosis (Boden 1998). I met Christine a few years later and corresponded with her for a time. Reference will be made to a remarkable conference talk that she gave (and subsequently published) later in this book. Given the seriousness of her situation, it is deeply moving that she should open her book by printing the following 'prayer' on the dedication page.

I asked God for strength that I might achieve;
I was made weak that I might learn humbly to obey.
I asked for help that I may do greater things;
I was given infirmity that I might do better things.
I asked for riches that I might be happy;
I was given poverty that I might be wise.
I asked for all things that I might enjoy life:
I was given life that I might enjoy all things.
I was given nothing that I asked for;
But everything that I had hoped for.
Despite myself, my prayers were answered;
I am among all (wo)men most richly blessed.[7]

The American Jeanne Lee (2003) decided that writing a book about her experiences might be of help to other people, and might be therapeutic for herself. She has written a small, easily read and very honest account of her life and her illness. "On a good day" she says, "I am still capable of writing a reasonably coherent letter, and yet other days I have a hard time constructing a single sentence". With help, she has written about her situation and has even opened up her own site on the internet! Speaking about the onset of her illness, which came when she was still relatively young, she describes how she felt:

I felt depressed and defeated. I tried to pick myself up for visits to the doctor, but otherwise I just stayed in the house and didn't do anything. I became a recluse. I was so ashamed of the way I talked. I felt stupid because I couldn't seem to put even a simple sentence together . . . the efficiency and organisational skills, which people once paid me for, had all but disappeared . . .

---

[7] Author unknown. Quoted by Christine Boden who acknowledges it as from '500 quotations for teachers and preachers', compiled by Robert Backhouse, Kingsway 1994

She manages to take quite a positive view of her life, and is determined that, although she is ill, she still has much to do and is still capable of doing a great deal – but –

> People just can't seem to understand that you can't re-learn things. There's something up there that doesn't come back, and you can't relearn and try to get better at it. It's just not there anymore. But it's not all gloom and doom. I can live with it quite nicely, as long as people don't expect too much and aren't constantly trying to convince me that there's nothing wrong. Don't try to teach me things I used to know and be good at, and don't over-protect, or act like it's some terrible thing that we should pretend isn't there.

Not everyone, of course, is a writer. These accounts are therefore, by their very nature atypical. In recent years there have been quite a number of research studies looking into how dementia affects people, how they understand it and respond to it (Crisp 1995; Keady Nolan & Gilliard 1995,Cotrell & Schulz 1993;Henderson 1998[8]; Gillies 1995; Clare 2002 ; De Baggio 2002– to name but a few)

The onlooker's perspective

There have also been a number of books written on the subject from the perspective of the carer. Let me mention just four of them to illustrate the view that people with dementia are unique individuals, with their own personalities and characteristics, as are their carers. It is dangerous therefore to make assumptions based upon one or two particular books, but taken together, they can provide us with a certain perspective which can be helpful as we seek to minister within this context.

---

[8] Writing in the Journal of Dementia Care (Vol 11 No 6) John Killick says of Henderson's book "Taken as a whole *Partial View* is the most successful attempt yet to present the world of a person with dementia experientially to the general reader"

Scar Tissue (Ignatieff 1993) is a semi-autobiographical novel by Michael Ignatieff describing the last years of his mother's life. There are some wonderful passages which depict the gulf in understanding or comprehension between the family member who sees the mother he loves and the clinical neurologist who sees a clear example of a specific disease; or his observation of the nurses. He writes that it was:

> as if some knew how to feel the pain of their patients without being frightened of it, while others felt they had to keep it at a proper professional distance;

an observation that could be made just as appropriately when observing how ministers, lay or ordained, relate to people with dementia. Incidentally, Michael Ignatieff spoke about his real mother with great love and insight during a discussion on the radio:

> I learned as much from my mother when she couldn't speak to me, when she couldn't communicate, when she simply stared and received our kisses on her cheek, as I learned when she was joking and laughing. What she taught me was that it's just an illness. It's a terrible illness, but it's just an illness. And there's life beyond the illness.[9]

James Nicholls was a professor at Princeton Theological Seminary in the States. His daughter Sue Miller is a novelist with many published works to her credit. In her book *The Story of My Father* (2003) she gives a graphic account of how she tried to come to terms with his diagnosis of Alzheimer's and his subsequent years of illness. She is honest about her dilemmas in caring for him, her mixed emotions and her struggle to confront her "terror of abandonment".

The novelist Iris Murdoch's illness and eventual death received a considerable amount of publicity. This was not just because she

---

[9] *All in the Mind* a discussion on BBC Radio 4, 1994

was one of Britain's leading literary figures but also because her husband John Bayley wrote a trilogy of three small books about their life together, about how they managed during Iris's illness and about how he coped after she had died (Bayley 1998, 1999, 2001). A film, *Iris*, was made with Judy Dench and Kate Winslett magnificently portraying the older and younger Iris. Opinion is divided as to how far the film furthered the cause of progressive dementia care, but there is no doubting that Judy Dench captured, in a remarkable way, the process of a deteriorating illness such as Alzheimer's.

There are many quotable passages in Bayley's tender books, but let me just take three as example of how, in this particular case, husband and wife learned how to find a way through their difficulties:

> One needs very much to feel that the unique individuality of one's spouse has not been lost in the common symptoms of a clinical condition . . . . .

> Our mode of communication seems like underwater sonar, each bouncing pulsations off the other, and listening for an echo. The baffling moments at which I cannot understand what Iris is saying, or about whom or what – moments which can promote anxieties, though never, thank goodness, the raging frustration typical of many Alzheimer's sufferers – can sometimes be dispelled by embarking on a joky parody of helplessness, and trying to make it mutual. Both of us at a loss for words.

> Alzheimer's, which can accentuate personality traits to the point of demonic parody, has only been able to exaggerate a natural goodness in her.

Remembering the formula that was spelt out in the last chapter – that dementia is a combination of a variety of variables – personality, general health, specific illness, biography or life history, the web of relationships, the physical sensory environment and a person's ethnicity: it should come as no surprise to find that someone else's experience of dementia is very different. Whereas in Bayley's case the illness brought the couple together in ways which reinforced their existing tenderness, and the illness 'exaggerated her natural goodness', for someone else the experience of dementia was very different. In *Remind me who I am again* (Grant 1998) the journalist and author Linda Grant describes just what her mother's illness meant to her; how she tried to cope with it and how she experienced it as a frustrating and bewildering process. Again, three quotations to give a flavour of the book and the experiences of a daughter:

> One of Multi-Infarct Dementia's cruellest tricks is to preserve in its victim until quite a late stage, some insight into what is going on in their mind, so that they can observe themselves lose their own sanity. Depression and emotional instability is a marked characteristic of this disease and who wouldn't be miserable watching themselves go mad ...

> ... The dogma is this: Social Services comply with what the elderly client wants. What does my mother want? It depends on which sense of herself is in the ascendant at any given moment and with each of these there is no memory of there being another self that wanted something else. What does the self I had come across crying on the toilet want? ...

> ... but she is so angry, so aggressive – she took me by the shoulders and pushed me out of the room, once, when I told her I didn't have the time to take her out. What Michele and I are after is a chemical solution. How about Prozac, the happy drug?

And that is how a great many people feel! Two very different accounts. But then, everybody's story is different because no two people have the same personality, the same personal history, the same web of relationships or the same pattern of health. An important principle in ministering to people with dementia and to their families is that we must endeavour to make no value judgements. We must recognise how unique every situation and every person is. There is much about the illness that we do not know. There is much about the person that we do not know and there is much about the nature of their pattern of relationships that we do not know. Somehow we need to approach each situation with an open mind and with no preconceptions, seeking only what is in the best interest of the person with dementia and then of their carers. Quite often these 'best interests' are in apparent contradiction and we have to learn how to live with such ambiguity without leaping to conclusions, to moral judgements or 'taking sides'. We also have to remember that we don't know how we would act if it were us who had the illness. Nor do we know how we would cope if we had to face the difficulties experienced by the carer in that situation. For of course, each carer too has their own distinctive history and pattern of relationships, their own personality and their own health problems.

Dementia poems

In recent years a new way into understanding the experience of dementia has been pioneered by the writer and poet John Killick. He has spent a great deal of time sitting with people with dementia, talking with them and writing down what they say to him. He then takes away all the things that they have said, sometimes clear and straight-forward and sometimes apparently gibberish or non-sensible. He then spends time reflecting on their words, and in many instances he can detect a theme, a meaning or an insight. Then, only using the words that the person has spoken he re-produces them in a quite remarkable way.

> Have you seen my barrow?
> I joined the group
> and now it belongs to all of us.
> But I don't know where it's gone.

It seems as if
I'm like a buzzing toy –
it buzzes round and round
but it doesn't mean much.

Altogether you won't find
much toing and froing
and doing or being
with me. I never carry
as full as you do.

The way this country's going
men can just go round
and do as they choose.
They can take my bed
and my barrow.

I think I just drift about.
I think that's what I do
usually. I'm just a kind
of quiet nobody. (Killick 1997a)

I have been at conferences where groups of professional workers
have sat down for an hour or more with some of John's poems.
The discussions that have arisen on these occasions have been
extremely interesting, confirming the view that there is a great
deal of insight and symbolism in them, and that they are very real
attempts to communicate what the person with dementia is
thinking and feeling. One of John's later books of dementia
poems (Killick 2000) has some fine black and white photographs
complementing the text. They could well be used as the basis for
meditation.

The 'stages' of dementia

It used to be quite common to talk about the '3 stages of
dementia', but many people are less sure about this now. The
pendulum has possibly swung because of too strict an adherence

to each stage, as though they were easily identifiable and discrete boxes through which people passed automatically. That clearly isn't the case. Dementia affects different people in different ways and at different speeds, and in any case, each 'stage' usually merges into the next in a very subtle and almost imperceptible way. I suppose it's rather like the transition from childhood to adolescence to adulthood; you know when a person is there, but you cannot with any certainty know when the transition actually took place, and even then there may be examples of behaviour appropriate to a different stage.

So whilst it may sometimes be helpful to talk about different stages, great care must be taken and we need to remember that these are only concepts that we are describing, designed to help us understand the situation better. The reality is much more complex. Cheston and Bender (1999) spell out a timely reminder:

> Stages, then, seemed to apply only to the general concept of dementia and not to particular people . . . He or she did not go through any stages - quickly or otherwise - because there were not any stages to go through.

Christine Boden (Boden 1998) commented that most of the literature describing the stages of dementia seemed to be written for the caregiver and she hadn't come across anything written for the person with dementia. In her book she therefore adapted something from the Alzheimer's Association in Australia and added her own comments. I am making a further adaptation of that!

Stage 1 is described as Mild and it may last for five years or so; sometimes for much less and occasionally for much longer. Christine says "we need you to be patient and understanding. I'm in this stage when I'm rested and well, and taking tacrine regularly".

- In this stage people may appear to be rather apathetic, showing less sparkle, but it may be because they are struggling to follow everything that is going on around them and are unsure if they have missed the point.

- They may show less interest in hobbies and activities that they previously enjoyed, perhaps because they now get tired much more quickly as their brain has to work harder to keep up.

- Some people may be able to keep up with the normal cut and thrust of conversation and everyday living, but may then need times of rest and solitude where they may seem to 'drift away'.

- They may find it harder to take new things on board and be unwilling to try new things, or adapt to change, because learning something new is very much more difficult and they may need much more help. Asking questions and needing things to be explained over and over again can become quite embarrassing and may lead to the carer becoming annoyed or impatient.

- People find it less easy to make plans or take decisions because to do so you need to be able to hold quite a lot of different types of information in your mind at the same time. This becomes more difficult for people with dementia. In much the same way, they find it more difficult to deal with complex issues because, as Boden says, "there is less storage space for ideas".

- There is sometimes a tendency to blame other people for 'stealing' their belongings. Because dementia brings problems with short-term memory, it is not uncommon for people with dementia to forget where they have put something and then to assume that someone has stolen it.

- People may become more self-centred, less concerned with other people and their concerns. This is because it takes much more of an effort to think about the needs of others, and also because the illness tends to diminish people's horizons. Also, some of the learned social niceties, 'good manners', may also be forgotten.

- Recent events or conversations may be forgotten very quickly; they have just failed to register within the brain.

- Very often people may repeat themselves, telling you the same thing time and time again. It takes an extraordinary effort to remember what is being said and done, and when the brain fails to take in this information the person with dementia has no remembrance of ever having said or done it.

Having said all that, because people are different and because the illness affects them in different ways, a person who has been diagnosed with dementia may not show any of these symptoms for quite a long time. A minority of people seem to be able to lead very full and creative lives for a long time after diagnosis, perhaps for several years. For them, the illness takes a different route and they seem to defy the conventional wisdom about dementia.

Stage two is described as Moderate and can last from about two to ten years. Christine Boden says of it "we need even more patience as well as subtle help, but please don't take over. I'm often in this stage when I'm tired or I've forgotten to take my tacrine".

- People with dementia may need assistance and supervision with certain tasks, such as getting dressed or using the telephone. Things which may have been totally routine in the past now seem to demand a great deal of thought and effort.

- People often become very forgetful of the recent past, but have clear recollections about the more distant past. This is because it is becoming more and more difficult for the brain to take-in and hold new information.

- People may become quite confused about what time it is, or what day it is. This can lead to situations where they may want to go shopping at midnight or they may have no clear understanding as to whether saying it is eight o'clock refers to eight in the evening or to eight in the morning. For most people, the brain automatically provides us with this sort of contextual information, but with dementia, this back-up system begins to disintegrate.

- When placed in unfamiliar situations or surroundings, people may very quickly become lost. Robert Davis wrote about his confusions when staying in hotels, and how he and his wife had to work hard at trying to establish which room was which and where different doors led to. Christine Boden speaks of how "everything looks so very different looking back than going forward". For many people, whether they have dementia or not, having a sense of being 'lost' can be extremely distressing, it can be all the more so for people with dementia.

- It often becomes more and more difficult to remember names and faces, and to fit them together correctly. This dislocation can then become tied in with a confusion about time and place, so that a friend of today might be thought of as someone from the past, or a daughter might be mistaken for a mother, a son thought of as a long deceased brother. Very often, at this stage, the person knows that they know you, but can't always associate the correct name or time or place. Christine Boden comments: "it is no longer important that you have a name, only that I know who you are". As the illness progresses, even that recognition may fade away.

- It becomes more and more difficult to do more than one task at a time. This becomes particularly clear in the kitchen, where saucepans may be left on the cooker, and gas or electricity left on. Fires may be left on, or gas appliances not lit. This can eventually become a health and safety hazard, not only for the person with dementia, but also for anyone else who may be living in the house. It is often situations such as this that lead to some sort of intervention by family members, neighbours or authorities.

▪ Quite often people with dementia are prone to wander. This can vary from walking, apparently aimlessly, for hour after hour, to quite determined and forceful walking. One lady in our church used to walk six or seven miles a day, winter and summer, round and round the streets. Sometimes people know how to get back home, often they don't. One day a scruffy bit of torn paper was pushed through my letter- box. On it were written the words "please help me I don't know where I am". Although the lady was lost, she could quite clearly remember that the Rectory was a place where she might find help. Unfortunately she didn't ring the bell and it was several hours later that we found the little note. A few years ago, one sunny afternoon, I found an elderly lady, dressed only in her nightie, walking around the garden. She had wandered away from a local nursing home, where frantic efforts were being made to find her.

▪ Another consequence of the illness, which often affects people, is that they begin to behave in inappropriate ways. One lady quite often persisted in standing up and singing out loud during the eucharistic prayer in a full church. Saying cheerio to people outside a church in the centre of Edinburgh one Sunday, a well-loved member of the congregation who loved her church but was finding it more and more difficult to concentrate and share in the worship in the 'normal' way, came out and screamed repeatedly that she hated Scottish people. This presented few problems to the worshippers, mainly Scots, as they left, but people passing by in the street raised an eyebrow or two! The possibilities for inappropriate behaviour, much more bizarre than these examples, are limitless.

- As the illness progresses, some people are convinced that they can see or hear things that no-one else seems to be aware of. John believed that each night, people from the television screen would walk through his house and Edna believed that someone in Wellington boots came into her flat, through the wall, every night. Some people are convinced that they are being robbed, others think that people are watching them. We have to remember that for the person with dementia, in their understanding, these things are actually happening, and no amount of argument or annoyance on our part will make them change their mind. Such behaviour and convictions require from us considerable insight, understanding and patience. They certainly do not require confrontation and disputation.

- Personal hygiene can be affected, as people forget to wash, or are sure that they have already done so. 'Accidents' can happen when the brain does not seem able to communicate that it is time to go to the toilet, and sometimes attempts to clean people up are physically resisted and deemed by the person with dementia to be some form of physical assault or invasion of their privacy.

The third stage, which is described as Severe can last for several years, probably for two to five, although it is always difficult to be precise about timings.

- The short term memory will have become almost non-existent and the person will have little recollection of what has just happened or what has just been said.

- Gradually the speech deteriorates and people become increasingly difficult to understand. Either because the words are apparently meaningless within the context or because they are no longer recognisable as words at all.

- There is the likelihood that the person will become doubly incontinent.

- There may be little or no recognition of family members or friends

- The person may need help with a great many tasks, such as washing, dressing, using the toilet or feeding.

- There may be a gradual decline in recognising the most common of objects, such as spoon or chair or telephone

- There may be disturbed nights (and disturbed days), a reluctance to co-operate with those who are caring for them, and occasional outbursts of violence

- Mobility may well decline markedly;

- The person may become permanently immobile and may be confined to bed until they slip into unconsciousness and in due time die. The mother of a friend of mine had been ill with Alzheimer's disease for over ten years. She had not known him for the last eight years and for the last six had been in a near-vegetative state. She had not spoken for six or seven years and each time he visited her she was curled up in a foetal position and that is how she eventually died.

It cannot be emphasised too strongly that not every person with dementia follows through these stages, nor are the experiences outlined above necessarily experienced in that order or in those particular stages. The idea of thinking in stages is a way of thinking about the progression of the illness, but it has obvious limitations and should only be regarded as a general tool to assist our understanding.

A different description of the progression of dementia, based upon the experiences of people with dementia has been set out by John Keady and Michael Nolan (Keady & Nolan 1994). They list nine distinct stages.

1. *Slipping* is the stage when a person begins to notice the occasional lapse of memory. These slips are initially ignored or discounted.

2. *Suspecting* is the stage when the lapses are too frequent to be dismissed and the person begins to suspect that something quite serious may be wrong.

3. *Covering up* happens when the person makes a quite deliberate attempt to disguise what is happening, another name for this is confabulation. This is often the stage where family members begin to suspect that something may be wrong. As the illness progresses, the person may seek to avoid those situations or conversations where their lack of competence might be noticed. One technique that Norman used was that he invariably asked people questions in order to get them talking and to minimise the amount of input that he was required to make in any conversation.

4. *Revealing* is the stage where the person confides to those who are closest to them, either voluntarily or after being confronted. But very often this information is kept within the close family and not shared with others.

5. *Confirmation* is the stage where there is an open admission that there is a problem and usually at this stage the process of diagnostic tests are made.

6. *Maximising* is when the person, knowing that there is now a progressive illness, learns new coping strategies and finds ways of compensating for their losses.

7. *Disorganisation* is when cognitive difficulties and behavioural problems are such that they become increasingly prominent. Fewer decisions are taken and the overall 'world' of the person continues to be reduced and diminished.

8. *Decline* is the stage when "any semblance of a normal and overtly reciprocal relationship becomes clouded and uncertain". Care giving becomes a dominant feature and there may well be admission into some form of residential or nursing care.

9. *Death* then becomes the final stage.

Various people (Kitwood 1990: Cheston & Bender 1999) have attempted to chart what it must be like for the person who has dementia; they have tried to suggest how a spiral of anxiety and depression forms as people move into these various stages of the illness:

Possible signs of early dementia emerge

▼

The person becomes aware of certain problems and losses

▼

After a period of time they recognise that they need some help

▼

Anxiety increases as various appointments are made and tests taken

▼

Further losses and problems are experienced, depression may set in

▼

Further assessments are made

There may be a loss of self-esteem & self confidence; more depression

▼

Greater anxiety and increasing depression are
superimposed upon decreased intellectual and memory functioning

▼

The person begins to accept and understand the diagnosis

▼

Further losses and problems are experienced

▼

There is a further increase in anxiety and possibly depression

▼

and so the cycle continues . . . .

At each of these stages there may be possibilities for creative intervention, for sharing and discussing, for planning and focusing on those things which still remain and on the contributions which the person can still make.

A small booklet *Don't make the journey alone* put together by people in the early stages of dementia has some encouraging things to say to others in a similar situation.(Alzheimer Scotland – Action on Dementia {AS-AD 2003}) "Being diagnosed with Alzheimer's disease is not the end of the world, whilst appreciating that things have changed, there's still a whole world to enjoy" writes Pat, and James comments "Dementia is not a major part of your life, just part of it. I don't waken up with my first thought being 'I have dementia!' I plan ahead and wake up thinking of the activities I have arranged to do that day". The booklet says that the authors dislike the word 'dementia' because they feel that it makes people look at them in a negative way, so they have tried to make something positive of the word in the following way:

D don't give up on life
E enjoy life, even with the restrictions
M make use of every minute
E eat sensibly
N now is the time to do all you've always wanted to
T try to cope by yourself but be prepared to ask for assistance
I insight – learn more about your illness and how to live with it
A act normally. It can be hard for others to spot: ask for assistance only when you must

The following short poem, written by a person with dementia, illustrates one person's way of coping. Whilst it may appear to be suggesting denial, I think it is really expressing how they have tried to come to terms with their situation:

Why am I so confused?
I can't seem to remember the things I should so
It seems like just yesterday everything was OK,
approaching the day in the usual way.
Today I forgot to eat my lunch.
Then I sat in the hallway
and thought I was on the bus.
Where am I going and where have I been?
Why am I in the constant state that I'm in?
What will the future bring in my case?
What will my mind tomorrow erase?
I mustn't think about it now,
it wouldn't do any good anyhow
I'll just pretend that everything is OK
and maybe tomorrow it will go away.   (Jansen 1999)

It is only in relatively recent years that people have been paying much attention to what the feelings and experiences of people with dementia actually are. As John Swinton (2001) puts it:

> When we ask the question *what does it feel like to have dementia* rather than simply *what is dementia* we begin to see this condition in a very different light . . . when viewed from the perspective of the person experiencing it, dementia is found to have 'hidden' (in the sense that they are not prioritised or noticed within the dominant biomedical discourse surrounding dementia) psychological and spiritual dimensions that are unnecessarily subsumed by the dominance of the medico-biological discourses.

Goldsmith (1994) commented that it was possible to view dementia care as a sort of pyramid, with the apex being inhabited by the medical experts, below them were professional carers, below them family carers and "the bottom layer of the pyramid is made up of people with dementia themselves. It seems to be a relatively novel idea to assume that they have a contribution to make, a voice to be heard." Work going on in the States in the late eighties and early nineties though, was trying to listen to how people with dementia perceived their illness (Cohen 1991). From our perspective, this interesting comment emerged from one man:

> Having Alzheimer's disease made me face ultimate realities, not my bank account. My money, job and other parts of life were trivial issues that restricted my growth, my spiritual growth. Alzheimer's disease transferred me from what I call the trivial plane to the spiritual or personal plane. I had to face the absolute horror of the A word, and I began a dialogue with my existence, a dialogue with my life and my death.

The fact that death is the final stage should not be interpreted as being the ultimate failure or as a sentence waiting to be pronounced. We all have to die and the challenge within dementia care is to work towards making the time between diagnosis and death as creative and fulfilling as possible. Although dementia is a devastating disability, it is not always and irrevocably a journey through hell and it is important that we find ways of supporting and encouraging people with dementia and their carers so that they can discover and enjoy a richness in life despite the limitations imposed by such an illness.

This can lead us once again into a reflection on the experience of the Exile in the Old Testament and to look once again at the significance of the road to crucifixion. There is a great deal within our tradition which can help us face up to an uncertain future. There is much in our tradition which grapples with issues of suffering and the struggle between hope and despair. The churches have much to contribute to the world of dementia care and dementia experience, but they need to be sensitive, compassionate and humble in their engagement.

Just as I am, I come
This is me Lord,
I hope you can remember who I am
            because I can't always put a name
            or face to me.
This is me Lord
I hope that you know what you are doing
            because I can't always,
            either for you or for me
This is me Lord
I hope you remember me
just as I am.
            'Just as I am, though toss'd about
            With many a conflict, many a doubt.
            Fightings and fears within, without,
            O Lamb of God, I come.' [10]

---

[10] From the hymn by Charlotte Elliott (1789-1871)

Chapter 5

Negative Experiences of Dementia

> Elderly individuals with dementia are among the most devalued members of our society, regardless of their lifelong characteristics and contributions . . . individuals who once fitted into the mainstream of society, demonstrating competence and productivity over their life span, now become marginal members within their immediate families and even more so within the larger social framework . . . the elderly demented individual bears the double stigma of age and mental handicap. (Lubinski 1991)

The negative view of ageing is as prevalent in our churches as it is within the wider society. How often have I heard people describe a congregation as 'just a group of old people', one minister even said to a colleague of mine that he didn't spend five years at university in order to work with a load of old people! Given this attitude towards ageing it is perhaps not all that surprising that people with dementia amongst the elderly are even more marginalized.

Of course, the experience of being discriminated against, of being shunned, is not confined to people with dementia, nor is it new; it is a universal experience. Often these experiences are similar to, or descriptive of, the experiences of people with dementia. Take, for instance, the situation of the nineteenth century poet John Clare, who spent many years in what was then called a 'lunatic asylum'.

I am – yet what I am, none cares or knows,
My friends forsake me like a memory lost,
I am the self-consumer of my woes,
They rise and vanish in oblivion's host.   (Clare 1997)

Words which have an uncanny resemblance to those of Psalm 22

My God, my God, look upon me; why hast thou forsaken me;
and art so far from my health, and from the words of my
complaint.
O my God, I cry in the day time, but thou hearest not;
and in the night-season also I take no rest . . .
But as for me, I am a worm, and no man:
a very scorn of men, and the outcast of the people.
All they that see me laugh me to scorn:
they shoot out their lips and shake their heads . . .
O go not from me for trouble is hard at hand:
and there is none to help me.
Many oxen are come about me:
fat bulls of Basan close me in on every side.
They gape upon me with their mouths:
as it were a ramping and roaring lion.
I am poured out like water, and all my bones are out of joint:
my heart also in the midst of my body is even like melting
wax.
My strength is dried up like a potsherd, and my tongue
cleaveth to my gums;
and thou shalt bring me into the dust of death . . [11]

When I was a boy, the word 'cancer' was hardly ever spoken.   A
discussion about cancer was conducted by whispers or knowing
glances.   Enormous changes have taken place over the past forty
or fifty years.   Now the majority of people are told their diagnosis
and they have the opportunity to become partners in the process of
treatment and, together with their family and friends they have the
chance to prepare themselves for whatever the future might hold.
We have not yet reached that state in dementia care.

---

[11] *Psalm 22* – selected verses. Book of Common Prayer version

Issues of diagnosis

There are a host of questions, practical and moral, to be addressed when thinking about whether people have been given a diagnosis of dementia (Fearnley, McLennan & Weaks1997). In terms of ministry we cannot be sure that people know much about their illness, some will and others won't. Also, because of the very nature of the illness some people may have been told a great deal about it and forgotten what they have been told. As time goes by we can expect that more and more people will have been given and shared a diagnosis, but at the moment we must assume that a great many people will not have been told much more than that they are 'having trouble with their memory'. Some families feel that there is stigma attached to a diagnosis of dementia and consequently they often seek to hide it from the person concerned and from friends and neighbours. As in other areas of ministry, great care and sensitivity must be exercised when such matters are raised.

One proprietor of a residential home told me that in his experience most people with dementia had received a late diagnosis (when the condition was already quite serious) and that they were never told what they were diagnosed as having. What he really hoped would happen was that people should have the opportunity of coming to terms with their illness, sharing the diagnosis with their family and friends and having the opportunity to plan and prepare for their future.

As diagnostic procedures improve, and new drugs are developed, it is to be hoped that people may be given a diagnosis at an early stage, when they have the time to think about it and discuss it; understand it and work out how they wish to prepare for the years ahead. Such planning can be very therapeutic in itself and can be a source of comfort for relatives. Having a person with dementia in the family can change the dynamics between people very considerably – a point that we shall be looking at in a later chapter.

The booklet *The Right to Know?* (Fearnley et al 1997) Concludes with these words:

> It is the right of the person with dementia to be given an early and accurate diagnosis, if he or she wishes, and information about the condition. Where there is an early diagnosis and both the person with dementia and the carer have the information they need, they are able to work together to deal with both the practical and emotional problems the illness brings. Access to the continuing support of an appropriate, skilled, professional practitioner is vital in allowing the whole family to find positive ways of living with dementia.

It is at times like this that sympathetic and sensitive ministry to and with a family can be of such importance and value. Because people are different, and everyone's situation is different from anyone else's, it is important that we do not rush into any sort of judgement. What may be the best thing for one person might not be the best for someone else. We must treat every individual and every circumstance as new and unique. People who are in the early stages of dementia may be feeling very vulnerable and to be told that they have an incurable illness may be extremely disquieting and destabilising. There is a right time and a right place – the theological *kairos*[12]- and authentic ministry is aware of this, either consciously or unconsciously.

So one of the negative experiences of dementia may be related to the way in which a diagnosis was (or was not) given. Fearnley et al (1997) outline some key principles and guidelines for good practice, suggesting that the diagnosis should be given by someone who has a good contact with the family and be seen as part of an ongoing process:

---

[12] There are two words for time in Greek. *Chronos* relates to chronological time –' 4pm on August 20th' for example, whilst *Kairos* refers to the right or appropriate time – 'it was time for a change' for example

- Choosing an appropriate setting for discussing the diagnosis
- Exploring how much the person knows already and how much they want to know
- Determining who else, apart from the patient is to be told
- Discussing the diagnosis
- Discussing the future
- Explaining what help is available
- Providing written information about the illness and also about sources of support
- Arranging a follow-up meeting for further discussion and support

Malignant social psychology

Moving on from diagnosis, Tom Kitwood, identified a whole range of experiences which he described as the 'malignant social psychology' of dementia (Kitwood 1997b). It is a chilling list when you read through it and probably we are all guilty, often for seemingly quite reasonable motives, of treating people with dementia in one or more of these ways. He points out that the losses that a person experiences because of their neurological condition are then followed by a change in people's relationships. Once a person has been diagnosed with some form of dementia, people then seem to think that that person is somehow 'different' and they begin to treat him or her in different ways – sometimes rather subtly and at other times quite blatantly. "People with dementia are subjected to a debilitating onslaught both from within and from the outside world."

- *Treachery* occurs when a person is told one thing when the other person knows quite well that something quite different is about to take place, or the truth has been manipulated in some other way.

- *Disempowerment* happens when people are not allowed to do things themselves which they may well be quite capable of doing. So the person with dementia is disempowered in two ways, first by the illness itself and second by other people's reaction to it and to them. When people realise that what happens to them may be independent of their responses they can 'learn helplessness', that is, they consciously or unconsciously 'switch off' and become helpless. Life is easier for them that way, their attempts to be independent having been squashed.

- *Infantilisation* describes the way in which some people treat people with dementia as though they were young children. They are not children, they are adults, and dementia is not a second childhood.

- *Intimidation* can happen when a person is subjected a barrage of tests or interrogation without really knowing or understanding what is happening or why.

- *Labelling* is what happens when someone is given a label, such as 'he's got Alzheimer's' and it is assumed that there is really nothing more to say; the label which has been attached to the person brings with it a whole host of preconceptions which may or may not have any relevance to the person with dementia.

- *Stigmatisation* is when a person is deemed to be somehow 'unclean' or 'less than a person' because of the nature of their illness.

- *Outpacing* occurs when people do not allow the person with dementia sufficient time to process the information that they are receiving and frame a response to it. We need to remember that, on average, it takes a person with dementia at least five times as long to respond. If they are not given sufficient time they are basically forced into quietness and isolation when, given time, they might still be able to share and contribute to conversations and activities.

- *Invalidation* is when a person's experience, opinion or belief is challenged or dismissed. It is not normally a helpful or appropriate thing to do to argue the 'facts' with a person with dementia. If that is the way in which they see and interpret the world then we need to discover ways in which we might be able to engage with them without invalidating their position. It can be extremely difficult to find ways in which to do this, but it is an essential and a worthwhile challenge for us to face up to.

- *Banishment* occurs when people make the assumption that the person with dementia is no longer with them and they proceed as though they didn't exist. There may come a time, of course when a person's disability is so severe that people have to get on with their lives but so often this happens long before it is either necessary or desirable. It is as though the person has been banished from their home, their family and their complex web of relationships.

- *Objectification* is the word used to describe the situation where the person with dementia is not spoken of or treated as a real person, with a unique identity, personal preferences, even a name. The person becomes 'he' or 'she' and is treated more as an object than a person. What Martin Buber would have called an *I-it* relationship rather than the preferable *I-thou*[13] relationship.

- *Ignoring* happens when life goes on as though the person were not there, conversations take place without any effort being made to include the person with dementia in them.

---

[13] Martin Buber (1878-1965) was a Jewish philosopher whose seminal book *I and Thou* provides much of the background thinking behind the present emphasis upon Personhood. See Goldsmith (2003) page 226.

When this happens the person invariably becomes even more isolated, making fewer efforts to communicate, and finding greater safety and less hurt in a withdrawn state. It is a vicious circle, slowly spiralling downwards.

- *Imposition* takes place when people are not offered choices or when their views are not sought – however difficult this may be – and things or events are imposed upon the person. This can range from deciding what they are to wear, to eat, where they are to sit, where there are to go and what is going to happen to them. Eliciting people's views can be a long and difficult process, but we now know from a whole variety of research studies that many more people with dementia can state their preferences about many more things than was thought possible just a few years ago.

- *Withholding* means that people with dementia are often not given information about their condition or about aspects of their care which, with careful attention being paid to communication, they might well be able to understand and express a view on.

- *Accusation* occurs when the person with dementia is blamed for something. The subjects about which they are accused can be as wide as blaming them for losing an item of clothing to being the cause of a person missing a bus!

- *Disruption* is when the person is seen as being a disruptive influence; this can vary from those occasions when their illness does in fact cause considerable disruption, to those occasions when they are just viewed as being 'potentially disruptive' and therefore related to in a particular way.

- *Mockery* happens when people make fun of the person with dementia, laughing at some of their strange ways and generally 'putting them down'. It is possible to laugh *with* a person – that is very different from laughing *at* them.

- *Disparagement* is when the person with dementia is spoken of in a deprecating, critical or belittling way. When that happens, they are being stripped of their personhood, treated as a non-being, as though they no longer had any value and were totally unaware of what was happening around them – a matter which is the subject of much thought and debate at the moment. If we treat a person as being a non-person, then the process of dehumanisation is affecting both of us.

We are facing a tremendous challenge when we set out to walk alongside the person with dementia. There are invariably many setbacks, many misunderstandings and moments of intense frustration and experiences of failure. If that is true for us, then what must it be like for the person who has the illness? We are also confronted by our own mortality and sometimes the only way that we seem to be able to cope is to protect ourselves by creating an invisible wall between ourselves and the person with dementia. It is part of the gospel imperative that we seek to break down those walls of division and discover and celebrate our common humanity. It can be a heart-breaking journey, but it can also be one full of rich and unexpected rewards and moments of insight and joyfulness.

> By the waters of Babylon we sat down and wept
> when we remembered thee O Sion . . .
> for how shall we sing the Lord's song
> in a foreign land?[14]

How? That is the question that we shall be attempting to answer as this book unfolds.

---

[14] Verses from Psalm 137

Despised and rejected,
a man of sorrows and acquainted with grief,
  betrayed, falsely accused, marginalised, mocked
  and taken away to die.
Lord, you have been through it all
  and that is why I can bring my breaking heart to you,
  for you understand,
  and you understand
  when I feel and think that God has abandoned me.
    "Be near me Lord Jesus
    I ask you to stay
    Close by me for ever
    And love me, alway"[15]

---

[15] From the hymn 'Away in a Manger' sometimes known as Luther's
Cradle Hymn. Authorship is unknown although it is thought that John
Thomas McFarland (1851-1913) wrote this verse.

Chapter 6

Communication and Dementia

When there are problems communicating with people with dementia, invariably the problems reside with the person who does not have the disability. That may seem a strange thing to say, given the fact that the varying illnesses behind the general term of dementia have such an effect upon a person's brain and upon its ability to take in, process and give out information. Nevertheless, there is now a vast amount of literature to suggest that, given time and skill, patience and commitment, it is possible to communicate with people with dementia for much longer than was thought possible only a few years ago. Perhaps the most significant feature in this new conviction about communication is that it occurs where the person without the disability believes that communication is possible. Without such a belief, there are a thousand reasons why we can convince ourselves that communication is impossible. I am not saying that it is possible for all people for all of the time, but that it is possible for far more people than we hitherto thought and for a much longer time. Granted, these times may be short and spasmodic and we may have to acquire and develop special skills to interpret and understand what is being communicated – but communication is possible.

Kate Allen (2001) spent several years doing research in this area, and she writes:

Things have been changing fast within the dementia world. Only five years ago the idea of asking people with this condition what they think about the services they use would have seemed at best misguided, at worst reflective of a basic misunderstanding of the reality of dementia. Images of disintegration, emptiness and loss predominated in thinking about dementia, as evidenced by book titles such as *The vanishing mind* (Heston and White 1991) and *Alzheimer's disease: Coping with a living death* (Woods 1989) and descriptions of the individual with the condition as 'an uncollected corpse' (Miller 1990).

Although public characterisations of dementia unfortunately persist in being highly nihilistic, and we all need to continue to challenge our negative assumptions, those who work directly with people with dementia are now operating in a very different culture. Through the published work of Tom Kitwood (1997b), John Killick (1997a; 1997b) and others, and the direct experience of many others, we are now at the stage of recognising and learning to engage with the unique, active and ongoing person, who continues to struggle to make sense of their world from within the condition.[16]

Perhaps nowhere else is the tension between the old and new cultures of dementia care more noticeably demonstrated than in the area of communication. It makes a huge difference if we regard the person with dementia as having an illness which makes them unable to communicate, unable to appreciate what is going on around them, and which slowly but inevitably turns them into a non-being – or whether we believe that the essential 'person' is still there despite the ravages of their disability. If we believe the latter, then we shall continue to search for ways of communicating, and of understanding just what it is that the person with dementia is feeling and perhaps trying to communicate. This is a great philosophical divide and one which should be of considerable importance to any community of faith, which believes that somehow, despite all our imperfections and limitations, we are moulded and shaped in the image of God, and are always, always, precious and valued in the mystery of the

---

[16] The letters following the dates for references have been changed to fit in with the overall referencing pattern of this book

Godhead. That we are, in the words of Eileen Shamy (1997), "more than body, brain and breath".

If the first prerequisite in communicating effectively with people with dementia is that we actually believe that communication is possible, in theory if not always in practice, then the second must be that we are prepared to respect the time and pace of the person we are communicating with. All people with dementia are different and they will respond and react in different ways, and so we must endeavour to personalise our approach and discover what 'works' for this person and what 'works' for a different person. There will be a whole range of variables for each person which affect their ability to communicate with us and we need to be aware of these. They include

- how the person is feeling – whether they are in pain or not

- how tired they are

- whether it is before or after a meal

- what they have been doing immediately before (were they over or under stimulated?)

- what time of day it is – some people are more able to communicate in the morning, others in the afternoon or evening

- how relaxed you are, whether you are in good eye contact, and whether the light is behind you or in front of you

- is there anyone else in the room?

- are there any distracting noises – is the radio or television on?

Gradually, over time, it should be possible to build up a general idea of when the most appropriate times and where the most appropriate locations are. It is a process which requires great sensitivity on the part of the carer, visitor or minister. It is also important that we do not lose heart when the going is difficult. There is no easy or sure route to success, but approached with patience, skill and sensitivity, there is every possibility that our efforts may bear some fruit. But our endeavours are not undertaken to bring us satisfaction, but to help provide a life-line and perhaps some consolation for the person with dementia. We do it for them, not for ourselves, but in the process we very often gain a great deal ourselves in the most unexpected of ways.

Some people seem to be born listeners, other people born communicators, and we can observe them with admiration. But even if we do not have those innate gifts, that doesn't mean that we cannot learn some of the techniques of communication, some little tips which might help us in this very demanding yet important work. The greater the severity of the disability the more we shall need those skills and techniques, and this is true even for those people who seem to have a natural gift in these areas. Tom Kitwood painted a graphic picture of the communicative process with a person with dementia. He said it was rather like two people on tennis court. The person with dementia plays the ball over the net and the other person has to be like a tennis coach and return the ball in such a way that the person on the other side can get to it and return it. The skill lies in knowing how to keep the ball in play, by returning it in such a way that the other person can continue the rally.

I have a wonderful photograph of my daughter holding my grandchild up, high above her head. They are both looking at each other and beaming with delight. They are equal partners in this activity, there could have been no photograph without the child, nor could there have been one without the adult. They need each other. But they are not equal in the sense that my grandchild is entirely dependent upon my daughter. She is in her care and she trusts her implicitly. In a similar way, the person with dementia is reliant upon others to maintain the conversation and to maintain a sense of security and continuity – but they remain partners in that process.

Some tips on communication[17]

Jane Crisp (2003) in an article written for nurses makes points which are just as relevant to people working with or visiting people with dementia in a local church context. She emphasises how important it is to reflect on how much you might know about the person and their present situation and what factors can be turned to advantage and what problems might be anticipated. She suggests that some of the points to be considered are

- the cultural, social and personal background of the person

- their name, and how they prefer to be addressed

- whether they have any further problems, apart from dementia

- what their daily routine is – and at which stage of it your visit may be taking place

Before going to visit a person, whether in their own home or in hospital or nursing home, it really is important that you prepare yourselves for the visit. If you cannot give the person your full attention because something else is on your mind, then postpone the visit. This is hard work and it needs all the resources that you have at your disposal. Make sure you have enough time, you cannot rush in and out of these visits, you need to know that you have some leeway at the end of what you might normally be expecting to be the end of the visit. Once there –

- don't rush things: communication takes time and you cannot hurry a person with dementia – to do so will almost certainly prove to be counter-productive. If you start a conversation you must have the time to let it develop

---

[17] Amongst various books on communication see Allen (2001), Goldsmith (1996), Lubinski (1991), Rau (1993) and the excellent Crisp (2000)

- it is important that you are not flustered, angry or that you have your mind on something else. Your 'body language' will almost certainly communicate your real state, even if your words don't

- give the person time to register that someone has arrived, don't immediately break into the activity or the silence

- introduce yourself by name, and perhaps by relationship – "hello mum, it's me, Johnny", or by some other identifying feature – "Hello Mrs Brown, it's me Douglas, from St.Mary's Church down the hill"

- be alert to how the person is feeling. You might not have arrived at the most convenient time, or you may have turned up when the person is not ready or able to communicate. Do not take this personally, it is probably nothing to do with you, although there is always an outside possibility that the person does not want to relate to you, either because of something you have said or done, or something that you represent, or because you remind them of someone else. You might be out of favour today but greeted warmly tomorrow, so you need to develop a certain 'toughness' so that you do not take any sort of rejection personally

- try to situate yourself at the same level as the person you are visiting; if they are sitting down, try to sit on a similar type of chair, if they are standing, stand alongside them, but not too close

- endeavour to establish eye-contact – but don't stare them out! A smile may say more than all the words you were thinking of saying

- speak slowly and simply, but do not speak down to them or patronise them. Some people speak about dementia as a 'second childhood', it is not, nor are people with dementia children, they are adults and deserve to be treated as such. They may have an illness which often gives the appearance of making them 'child-like' but they are not 'childish' and to treat them as children can, in extremes, become a form of abuse

- allow the person time to process what you have been saying. It can take up to five times as long for a person with dementia to hear, process and perhaps understand what you are saying, so pace your words carefully

- try not to use long and complex sentences. Only deal with one thing at a time, for example, instead of saying 'would you like a cup of tea and then go out for a walk', divide that into two separate exchanges. 'Would you like a cup of tea?' (Yes – No)   'Would you like to go out for a walk?' (Yes – No)

- it often helps to provide people with choices rather than using open-ended questions. So you might say "would you like fish and chips or a salad for tea?" rather than "what would you like for tea?"

- do not be afraid of touch, it can be a powerful form of communication, but do not encroach upon a person's personal space if they are clearly uncomfortable with touch. Many people may value your sitting with them and holding their hand as you converse. Other forms of touch which are often appreciated are brushing a person's hair or applying cream or lotion to their hands or face. Clearly, this is appropriate for some people to do and not for others, depending upon the relationship. The important thing to grasp is that it is not necessary to use words in order to communicate

- do not be afraid of long pauses, the person may be in the process of absorbing what you have said, and try not to jump in and provide 'answers' or complete sentences for them. Remember, the whole process of conversation will take much longer than with a person who does not have this illness. That should not be used as an excuse for not taking the time to communicate with them and for making decisions on their behalf which they might well be competent to make for themselves, given a little time and support

- the fact that someone may not answer you straight away, or even at all, may not necessarily mean that they have not understood you. It may mean that, of course, but it may also mean that they are choosing not to respond (do we know why?), or that they want to respond but don't know how to (are we sensitive enough to the situation to be able to discern if that is the case?).

Jane Crisp (2000) recounts a wonderful story coming from a French psychologist and psychotherapist

A well-known professor was applying some clinical tests to a female patient to determine how advanced her dementia was. He ordered her to 'lift the left hand', 'shake the right leg', 'give my hand a good squeeze', etc. but he got no response. Instead, the patient became agitated and made us understand that she wanted to go to the toilet. Once there, much to my amazement she confided to me 'He really irritates me, that stupid bearded chap with his silly questions. I'll stay here so that he gets irritated and pushes off!' Incidentally, this woman patient had always disliked bearded men!

Developing a technique

Dementia care is part science and part an art form. There are things that can be learned, and it is important that we learn as much as possible. But there are also aspects that cannot be learned. I suppose that intuition is the best way of describing what I mean. Some people just seem to have the 'knack'. They may be highly qualified professional people, or they may be the most simple and unsophisticated of people, but somehow, they just seem able to communicate. Ideally we need both, together in one person if at all possible. But for all of us, whether we have a natural aptitude or not, there are certain basic things that we can learn and be aware of, such as the preceding list of tips. Together with this, we need to develop what can only be described as a 'poetic awareness'. To realise that words may be symbolic, metaphors for a reality that may not at first be obvious. Kitwood (1990b) puts it this way:

> We need to slow down our thought processes, to become inwardly quiet, and to have a kind of poetic awareness; that is, to look for the significance of metaphor and allusion rather then pursuing meaning with a kind of relentless tunnel vision.

I have already mentioned the work of John Killick (1997a, b), who crafted the exact words of the people with dementia that he was visiting and created an art-form from them. In the poem below he thinks that the speaker "seems only to be able to conceive of his existence in terms of a catalogue of all the objects that he has known. He is obsessed with the material nature of the world. Or is it that, lacking the capacity any longer to follow a logical train of thought, he has fallen back upon free association, for sometimes there appears to be a linking principle, but as often it is some intuitive resemblance, or even the sound of a word that suggests the next link in the chain of meaning."

I used to play the arpeggios and the overtures.
My brother Jack would sing it straight off
'Will o' the Wisp', 'Whispering'.
And then you've got 'The Birth of the Blues'.

You've got Mutton Chops, Pork Chops, Pork Dripping,
Lard, Margarine, Butter, Butter Beans.
Now Marjorie grew some beautiful flowers
In her greenhouse. And tomatoes too.

You've got your Sunlight Soap, Saline Drip, Crumpsall Biscuits,
Crimplene, Cashews, Rose-coloured flowers –
I used to take a bouquet of a dozen roses
To my mother when she had the babby.
You've got Sun Shades, Unbrellas, Lemonade
(great big bottles), Butterscotch, Scotch Whisky –
When my Uncle Albert was top public
He won a Scholarship, pure thoroughbred.

There's Brass Bands, Cornets, Wafers, Blocks
Choc Ices, Whipped Cream Walnuts, Boxes of Dairy Milk –
My mother would buy a quarter a week,
And my father had one ounce of plug tobacco.

You've got your Beddings, Nottingham Lace Curtains,
Carpets, Woollen Blankets, Wooden Tops, Turnip Tops,
Spinning Tops, Trampolines, Heavy Mattresses, Beds that
When you put your fet down you get cold ones at the end.

Bandages, Band Aid Clubs, Puttees, Putting Greens,
Flags of all the Nations, Hat Pins, Pin Tables,
Plus Fours, Pincers (with their Movements), Pliers,
Planks of Wood, Woodchoppers (with their Balls) ....

I never felt so well – it's the laughter,
It keeps me young, it beats all the drugs.
I've always told the truth. And in this
That has truly been my intention.   (Killick 1997a2)

Jane Crisp has this 'poetic awareness' in abundance and her book
Keeping in Touch with someone who has Alzheimer's (2000) was
written following her mother's illness. It is a minefield of insight
and awareness, written in a style that is easily accessible and
designed to be of help and support to others in similar
circumstances. She has good things to say about how we can try
to make sense of their words by looking for links and recognising
words from the past. 'Keep Listening' she urges. 'Words are

rarely meaningless'. She then sets out ways by which we might be able to understand their stories, and counsels that we should not automatically assume that a story is untrue because, taken on face value, we know that it cannot have happened or because it is made up of such a strange mixture of ingredients. Working closely with her mother, she clearly was able to make out meaning from words and stories which most other people might have regarded as the nonsensical language of Alzheimer's. It is all a matter of poetic awareness.

Varieties of communication & varieties of ways of communicating

Communication does not have to take the form of two people sitting down and conversing face to face. There can be many variations on that theme. Nor does it need to be verbal, there are many other ways of communicating. Indeed, there can be much that is communicated by a shared silence, a sitting alongside one another without need for words. Facial expressions, a gentle touch, a shared activity – all can be means of communication.

There can also be wonderful opportunities for sharing, and for sharing words, whilst going about the routine and daily tasks, such as washing, dressing, toileting and the like. These are occasions when the focus is not upon speech and therefore the person with dementia may be rather more relaxed and not concentrating on trying to remember words or follow conversations. Instead of seeing these tasks as routine chores, we should try to see them as opportunities for closeness, touch and perhaps conversation that are not granted to us in the normal run of things. If we can see them in this way, it might even make some of the more humdrum aspects of dementia care seem more worthwhile, perhaps opening up opportunities hitherto closed or closely guarded.

Creating a scrapbook

Many people have found that compiling a scrapbook of pictures and reminders of a person's life has been a valuable way of spending time together and providing opportunities for reflection and conversation. Photographs of the towns (or countries) that the person has lived in, reminders of work that they may have been involved in, family photographs and reminders of holidays or hobbies and clubs that they may have belonged to, can all be imaginatively presented. It is often a good idea to provide a simple text alongside the pictures, such as a note of where the place is or of who the person is. This can be of help to other people who may share time with the person looking through the book.

Local churches might build up their own scrapbooks, showing pictures of the building and photographs of members past and present together with reminders of special events in the church's year or of special Festivals such as Christmas or Easter, when the church might be decorated in a seasonal way. If there is a page showing the church at Christmas, it might be an idea to print a verse of a carol to stand alongside it. That could serve as a prompt to talk about other carols, or their favourite carol. It might even lead to a little singing. It is an interesting fact that many people are still able to sing songs even when normal speech seems to be difficult. Scrapbooks are probably best presented in polythene folders, or even laminated, as some people with dementia often tear loose pages.

If the person eventually goes into some form of residential care, then not only are such scrapbooks of value to the person and their visitors, they can also provide many helpful clues and cues for the care staff. Assembling such a scrapbook can be a pleasurable activity for the whole family, and one in which the person with dementia may well be able to share in. Photographs of family members, taken over the years, can be a source of endless comment, giving rise to many memories that can be shared and talked about. Compiling such scrapbooks is now much easier as so many people have access to computers and to digital photography.

Building up a Memory Box

A memory box is rather like a three-dimensional loose-leafed scrapbook. It can be of any size, but probably something the size of a shoebox is easiest to manage. The idea is to place in the box up to a dozen items which may have particular significance and meaning to the person with dementia (Treetops 1996, Hammond 2002). It may be something that you can create together, and it is certainly something that people in the early stages of dementia can think about. What different people put in their box will be as varied as the people themselves. It could be a stone from the garden which they love, it could be an ashtray that they won at Blackpool fifty years ago, it could be a special photograph, the service sheet of a daughter's wedding, a particular piece of jewellery, a favourite pipe, a regimental badge or a programme from a particular football club – anything, which might evoke special and cherished memories.

A memory box is something that the person may dip into when they are alone, looking at, feeling and thinking about the various items. No words are needed. Or it can provide a topic of conversation when visitors come. In fact building up a memory box is an exercise that anyone can do, and it is probably quite a therapeutic process for all of us. From the vast number of your possessions, what ten or twelve articles would you want to hold on to if you were to lose all the others. It is a sort of Desert Island Discs, but with a much greater significance than entertainment.

'Life Story' work

It does not matter that, as a young girl growing up in Boston, Massachusetts, she helped to raise her seven brothers and sisters and that she took care of her elderly mother. It does not matter that she once was able to fix plumbing, hang wallpaper and prepare a full dinner every night, while keeping her six kids out of major trouble. It does not matter that she once could swim faster than anyone in her family, that she secretly yearned to be a basketball star, that her late husband considered her the most beautiful woman he'd ever seen . . . . (Kantrowitz 1989)

One of the saddest consequences of people having dementia is that people so rapidly forget or ignore all that a person has done and achieved; or perhaps they have never known. Even more sad, is the fact that, not knowing, many people involved in caring for people with dementia do not take the trouble to find out about the life of the people who now so often present themselves as frail and vulnerable. Many of them have been giants, with rich and rewarding lives, causes for celebration and thanksgiving. Those who have struggled, apparently achieving little apart from survival against all the odds in a life which may have been hard, sad or even tragic, perhaps need even greater understanding, sympathetic companionship and support as they face this latest challenge.

Charlie Murphy (1994; 1997) has written about the value of building up a person's life story. One carer wrote to me: "with my mother we produced a 'This is Your Life' photo album. It was a prized possession, shared with every visitor. She herself used it as a memory jogger – it allowed strangers an insight into her background and allowed communication with less expenditure of effort on her part and retained her memories for longer than would have been otherwise." A variation on this theme from a church perspective would be to create a Thanksgiving Book in which a person reflects upon all the good things and all the blessings that they have experienced over the years. If this is done in the early stages of a person's illness it could be a rich resource to draw on as the time passes. Being involved in a creative activity like this might prove to be an easier way of communicating and sharing than just sitting down and engaging in a face to face conversation. It might, quite clearly, take a long time to produce, but that does not matter. Nor does it have to be a physical 'book', there are many other ways of recording memories. Nor does it matter if it never gets finished. The important thing is that it has enabled the person with dementia to share in an activity which involves communicating with others, and which also turns their mind and memory to good and happy experiences rather than reflecting upon what they have lost or fear that they are soon about to lose.

Telling the story of one's life has been likened to weaving a tapestry with the symbolic ribbons of family, friends, faith, hope, experience, sorrows, joys and much, much else. Jill Ison called it (1998) "a weaving of great beauty, significance and holiness".

Conclusion

It is difficult to exaggerate the importance of communication in the world of dementia care. As Anne Whitworth and colleagues put it (1999):

> The ability to communicate is central to social life, and the opportunity to engage in social interaction provides a powerful means for defining self, achieving self-esteem and maintaining relationships with others. The breakdown of communication in dementia has a devastating effect on both people with dementia and their families as the mechanism to maintain their relationship is compromised... by a breakdown in language processing, a breakdown in motor speech production or a breakdown in other cognitive processes.

People in churches should not need to be reminded of the importance of communication because in many ways they are deeply involved in the communication business. Hopefully this can show itself in a willingness to take seriously the very real problems that many people with dementia and their carers face, and to work patiently and with commitment to ensure that we develop the skills of listening, encouragement and interpretation.

It is not an easy task, but it is an extremely important, indeed compassionate, task.

Open my ears that I may hear
Open my eyes that I may see
Open my heart that I may have compassion
Open my mind that I may have understanding
Open my hands that I may touch
Open my arms that I may embrace
Open my imagination that I may try new things,
    then Lord,
Open my mouth that I may speak

Chapter 7

Family Carers

It is now over twenty years since the important book on caring at home for confused elderly people *The 36 Hour Day* was written (Mace & Rabins 1981)[18], dedicated to "everyone who gives a '36-hour day' to the care of a person with a dementing illness". A quote from the Foreword sets the scene by describing a not uncommon experience:

> . . . .the patient may be preoccupied with her bowels or with waiting for her long-deceased husband to return from work to eat the meal she has prepared for him. The patient's daughter (and I make no apology for casting both patient and carer in the feminine role, because this is as it is in the majority of cases) is pre-occupied with how much longer the patient will exhaust and torment her with outrageous behaviour, and how much longer she will be able to bear it; with what is going to happen next; with what caused it all; with whether she will suffer the same thing herself in her own old age.

I have deliberately started this chapter off with a rather bleak scenario. It was clearly written before Kitwood's 'new culture of dementia care' was widely known and in many ways quotations like the one above echo some of the despair expressed by Robert Davis's wife in *My journey into Alzheimer's disease* and Linda Grant in *Remind me who I am again*. But *The 36 Hour Day* is a realistic and practical guide to help, support and encourage the many people who looks after their relatives at home. It is estimated that there are over 5.7 million informal carers in the

---

[18] The revised UK edition was published in 1985, references here relate to the UK edition with alterations and 'translations' by Beverly Castleton, Christopher Cloke and Evelyn McEwen

United Kingdom, with half of those caring for someone over the age of 75 [19]. No matter how much love and commitment there is, it is still a long, hard and extremely tiring occupation that has been placed upon people without their asking for it or being prepared for it.

So how are family carers affected?

- they have much less time for themselves and for other members of their family

- there are usually adverse financial implications, either because they may have had to give up paid employment or because of an increasing amount of incidental expenditure

- they undergo considerable stress and may become unusually worried, nervous, tense or irritable. Burns and Rabins (2000) write that compared with non carers, they are more likely to take prescribed medication, visit their GP more often (by 50%) and report higher levels of stress and physical sickness.

- if they are not in good health themselves, then their condition may well deteriorate

- at some stage, and for long periods, they are likely to suffer from chronic fatigue brought on by lack of sleep and reduced opportunities for rest and recreation. Research has suggested that there is a significant association of depression and anxiety if the carer is a woman over 65 years old, being a co-resident and next of kin to the person being cared for (Cooper et al 1995)

- they may well experience feelings of anger, guilt, shame and despair. Sometimes feeling overwhelmed by sadness,

---

[19] Office of Population Censuses and Surveys 1995

often feeling misunderstood, and frequently feeling under-valued and unappreciated

- their own quality of life often deteriorates markedly and their sense of satisfaction with life can easily diminish

- there is often an increase in family conflict, and

- they can lose contact with their friends, with their work colleagues, with their hobbies, outside interests and their church and feel themselves increasingly trapped by their circumstances and within their homes.

Jacqueline Kinsey Bamberry (1997) described her experience of caring in this way:

As he entered the last two horrifying months of his life I could barely sustain my inner strength. I felt that emotionally I was unravelling and disintegrating. I was conscious of a void filled only with pain and terror. I entered an alien and foreign place.

I don't know if the person here had dementia, but that is not the point at issue, the quotation is used to describe the draining effect of caring. That will not be everyone's experience of course, some people will feel an immense sense of relief, completion and wholeness when death eventually approaches, though often tinged with a sense of guilt that they should feel that way. The experience of carers is as different as the carers themselves, but they certainly do have experiences and the good pastoral minister is alive and alert to them. The novel *Family Matters* by Rohinton Mistry (2002) beautifully illustrates the implications and burden of caring for an elderly relative and the ways in which other family members inevitably become involved.

Stages of caring

Carpentier and Ducharme (2003) argue that caregivers pass through four definite stages, not of equal length, nor necessarily all that distinct, but nevertheless identifiable.

- There is the time when they begin to recognise early symptoms. For quite some time they may have kept this to themselves before sharing their observations and concern with the person concerned. They will probably have been met with denial and perhaps anger before, eventually, there being some acceptance that perhaps there might be some value in getting some outside advice, usually from their doctor. This can last for a year or two.

- They then have to come to terms with the diagnosis and endeavour to find out as much as they can about what this illness is all about. People's experiences with GPs vary enormously, but there is often a criticism that the diagnosis comes too late (Downs 2002). People are not always told what is actually wrong with them (recognising that diagnosis can be very difficult) and often they are confused as to what they have been told. Hopefully though, a person will have been given a clear diagnosis, together with supporting literature and various contacts which may be able to provide ongoing support and encouragement. This then should be followed up shortly afterwards, to see how well it has been understood, and a general plan of action suggested and agreed. There is therefore quite a lot to be digested, discussed and understood during this second stage of caring. Some carers are very reluctant about the diagnosis being given to the person with dementia. They seek to 'protect' them; but increasingly the view is being accepted that it is right and proper that a person should be given their diagnosis, thus giving them the time and opportunity to think about things and possibly to plan ahead. GPs differ considerably in their ability to diagnose and communicate, and patients differ considerably in their capacity to take on board the reality of their diagnosis, so there are always going to be blurred edges.

- The third stage is usually the longest and the most draining. It is the time of providing care at home, the time when there will a great deal of "perseverance and resignation". As much of this chapter is concerned with this third stage, I will not expand on it here, apart from saying that it can last for several years.

- Finally there is the stage when problems of institutionalisation have to be faced. This can refer to the almost automatic responses that sometimes develop when being cared for at home, when some people find it almost impossible to experience any sort of relationship. More generally though it refers to the stage when carers reach the often difficult and painful decision to place the person with dementia into some form of long-stay care, be it in a nursing home or hospital. This is often a desperately difficult decision, evoking a whole range of emotions from grief to relief, from guilt to a sense of completion. It is usually a decision that has been wrestled with for a very long time, unless it has been precipitated by a fall or by some illness, either on the part of the carer or of the person with dementia. Invariably there are problems relating to the institution chosen, the principal one being that it is not "home". The carer has to bear the burden of this new set of problems, just as some of the other ones are being lifted.

- I would like to add a fifth stage, that is the stage of coming to terms with the death of the person. Coping with the death of a relative, especially if that person is a spouse or a parent is invariably difficult. These difficulties are often accentuated if the person died having dementia. It is even more problematic if the person was young. I shall discuss these points in greater detail later on.

Why caring for people with dementia is so demanding

Signposts to Support (AS-AD 2003b) is a very useful publication aimed at understanding the special needs of carers of people with dementia, and in its second chapter it identifies ways in which the very nature of the illness makes caring so specifically different from caring for people suffering from many other illnesses. It reminds us that for most carers of people with dementia their own knowledge and understanding of the illness prior to a diagnosis being given will be very limited and that they will be unprepared for what is likely to follow. The fact that people are all so very different, that the illness takes people in different ways, and that the time scale can be rather erratic and prolonged, all combine to add to the burden of caring. The reasons why caring for people with dementia can be so demanding, especially as the illness progresses, can be summarised in this way:

- there is an increasing need for intimate personal care as the illness progresses and this can be difficult for some children to give to their parents (or to their in-laws)

- as time goes by, the person will need increased assistance in tasks like washing, getting dressed, feeding, and preparing for bed. Some of these tasks can be physically very demanding, particularly if the carer is elderly or not in good health

- as the person's ability to carry out everyday activities diminishes, so increased supervision is needed. This is particularly true when outside trips are taken and when the person with dementia is in a public place

- carers increasingly provide emotional support for the person with dementia, and this can be very difficult and wearing if the person's mood swings are marked or if they experience extreme anxiety, depression or anger. It can sometimes seem like living on the edge of a volcano, not knowing whether or when it is likely to erupt. They have to cope with behavioural changes which may include disinhibited social behaviour. During all this they have to remember that these moods and actions are the consequence of an illness, of a deterioration in the activity of the brain, and try not to become angry or accusing

- gradually it will be necessary to take over the decision-taking in matters relating to finance (which may be something completely new to the carer) and other major issues

- there may well be risks to the safety of the person with dementia, and to others, because of forgetfulness (such as leaving the gas on) or because of acts of reckless behaviour (John Bayley writes of the time when Iris Murdoch opened the car door and jumped out whilst he was driving)

- there may be considerable personality changes, and the person that the carer has known for many years may suddenly seem to become 'a different person'. Mild people may become aggressive, active people may become very apathetic and so forth:

> My mother has cursed more times in a month than I had heard her curse in an entire lifetime – is this the same person I once knew, the same person who was always very careful to control her anger.... this disease challenges and relativises all of our assumptions about language, meaning and humanity itself (D. Keck 1996)

All this can be extremely wearing and debilitating for the carer. Of course, from the perspective of person-centred care we are wanting to emphasise the belief that the person has not fundamentally changed, and we have to remember that changes are taking place in the brain because of their illness and that this makes them behave in different ways, just as a person who has a damaged leg may develop a limp. I know that it is a thousand times more difficult to cope with than a damaged leg, a million times more difficult, but the person remains. On top of all the other challenges facing the carer, there is this ultimate challenge of still believing in the person.

- there will almost certainly be consequent changes in the nature of the relationship, and a diminution of the quality of life for the carer.

If the carer is a spouse, then as the dementia progresses the marital relationship will almost certainly become increasingly unbalanced {according to de Vugt et al (2003)}. As the illness progresses, the quality of the relationship and the level of intimacy tend to deteriorate, enjoyment of each other's company diminishes, communication becomes more difficult and reciprocity is drastically reduced. Interestingly, de Vugt found that when people's behaviour was disruptive, this was seen as less of a threat to the relationship than those situations where the person with dementia lapsed into apathy and became more and more difficult to make meaningful contact with. It is as if the disruptive behaviour at least gives the carer something to engage with, distressing though it might well be. They write:

caregivers are better able to cope with excessive behaviour that disrupts interaction than they are with a decrease in interaction because of diminished conversation or disinterest on the part of the patient.

Having recognised how the relationship may diminish, it is interesting to note than many of the people who shared these views with researchers also admitted that, paradoxically, at the same time they also felt closer to their spouse than in the past. This is particularly true of the early stages of the illness and the reasons given for this were:

- the fact that both the person with dementia and their partner had come into this situation together, and together they had had to come to terms with the diagnosis of dementia

- sharing these difficulties in many ways strengthened the bond between them

- they recognised that the quality of their relationship could no longer be taken for granted, and they become determined to enjoy the time that they have left together, and

- the caregiver inevitably tends to become more protective of the person with dementia and this can make them feel closer even though daily interaction becomes more difficult.

Judith Scott (2001) wrote this poem '*Letting Go*' as she reflected on her relationship with her mother who had advanced Alzheimer's.

> I tried to imagine how you felt
> Incredibly frightened, yes, but
> Also
> So bitterly angry and frustrated
> By the things you couldn't do,
> That just – WOULDN'T – be done
> No matter how hard you tried.
> The words that wouldn't come
> When you so wanted to put a
> Good face on things
> The way your mind let you down
> And forgot what you were doing
> Where you were going
> And why.

That anger spilled over into everything
And blazed out against everyone.
I did understand, and grieved that
There was so little I could do:
You fought me as if I was the devil himself.
Accused me, abused me, rejected me
When I tried to help.

I knew it was the disease you hated,
Not me. The doctors said it would be easier
When you stopped fighting it, so
I prayed for that day to come,
But I didn't realise how it would be –
Not easy at all – to see you finally accept
Defeat and give in. And I didn't know
how I would weep, to see you,
Letting go.[20]

Sex and dementia

As in so many other areas, it is extremely difficult to generalise
and individual couples will have their own ways of sharing
intimacy, but sadly, even these are invaded by the progressive
illnesses that we are thinking about:

> Although this is an area that is often fraught with difficulties,
> it must be recognised that for many people with dementia,
> physical contact and sexual activity with someone whom they
> love can provide those moments of intimacy that are of
> enormous significance and value. Words are not needed and
> the reality of the distressing illness can, for a time, subside.
> (Goldsmith 2003)

---

[20] I found this poem on the internet and have made great efforts to track
down the author to seek her permission to quote it, but so far to no avail.
The e-mail address I have come across several times no longer seems to
be valid.

The fact that a person is growing older and has a dementing illness does not necessarily mean that they do not have sexual needs. Indeed, some people with Alzheimer's disease often display increased sexual activity (Derouesne et al 1996). If these needs are ignored and not dealt with honestly and creatively there is the likely probability that they will reassert themselves in other forms of behaviour which might be equally or even more difficult to cope with. Of course, some people lose much of their sexual appetite and it becomes one of the many things which seem to sink within an overall context of apathy and disinterest. Partners too have sexual needs and how carers address those needs is a complex and sensitive subject. These problems are highlighted and even more important when the person has early-onset dementia and may still be within their forties or fifties.

Bright (1997), discussing sexuality and people with disabilities (in which category she places people with dementia) draws on work done by Litz (et al 1989) and says that the partners of people with Alzheimer's disease are often unhappy about sexual relations for a whole number of reasons, but chief amongst these are –

- because the partner with dementia may forget what to do to achieve intercourse, or

- because they make inordinate demands for intercourse, having forgotten an incident earlier in the day, or

- because the spouse feels uncomfortable with the idea of having intercourse with someone who cannot remember his or her name, or remember that they have been married for many years.

Sherman (1998) has identified five areas in which we might expect to discover certain problems, and Carole Archibald (1994, 1997), and Haddad & Benbow (1993) have explored some other important themes

- problems with sexual modesty, which may range from telling dirty jokes at inappropriate times and in inappropriate places; divulging sexual intimacies from their life to strangers or friends; making suggestive comments or failing to dress appropriately

- problems with specific sexual behaviours which may cause offence or embarrassment to others and certainly to their carers

- changes in sexual patterns in marriage

- effects of behaviour changes on family members, who may find it both embarrassing and perplexing; there may be demands for curbs and restraints from some of the family or the urge to 'put the person away'

- illicit relationships, especially if the person lives in some type of residential care. There are many stories of families being surprised or hurt when their relative appears to be developing some sort of relationship with someone else in the home. Situations occur such as a wife bringing a gift to her husband who then goes and gives it to his 'lady friend', apparently unaware of his relationship with his wife. These situations can raise enormous moral dilemmas for members of staff in such establishments – are they required to act *in loco parentis?* (Seeber 2001; Barker & Wattis 1991)

Sherman points out that the reasons behind these types of behaviour may be as a result of further damage within the brain, the consequence of drugs that they might be on, or they may be an expression of boredom or frustration with their present situation and a feeling that their opportunities for pleasurable enjoyment are diminishing. Whatever the reason, many carers find the whole area of sexuality and dementia a difficult one to come to terms with. What will happen when people who are sexually active in our present permissive culture grow older and perhaps get dementia we do not yet know, but one can hazard a guess that a few new demands for understanding and imaginative care may be called for.

There are particular problems posed by gay and lesbian people with dementia, who are marginalised on account of both their illness and their sexuality. These problems are only just beginning to be addressed. It is a sign of encouragement though that these matters are now being brought into the public domain and dealt with sympathetically (even if only in a very few places at the moment). It has been estimated that perhaps one in fifteen service users is either a lesbian or a gay man but their views, and those of their carers, remain largely unrecognised (Ward 2000)

Our churches do not have a good track record in helping people come to terms with their sexuality, whatever it may be, and affirming them. For too long sex has been the great taboo subject within churches and the slightest aberration or imagined aberration in the field of sexual conduct creates greater disturbance and receives greater condemnation than a thousand other peccadilloes be they major or minor. Many people with dementia and their carers may well feel that they have strayed beyond the acceptance of the church because of problems of sexual behaviour resulting from dementia, or because of their own sexuality. It will take a great deal of time and patience, understanding and repentance (on the part of the church) before this situation is rectified.

When care at home is no longer feasible

There are three main reasons why some people with dementia move into some form of residential care. Two are relatively straightforward and the other may be quite problematic:

- when the person with dementia has an accident or falls ill and they are no longer able to cope or live independently or with their principal carers

- when their principal carers have an accident or fall ill

- when their principal carers feel that they can no longer continue caring within the community because of exhaustion, too many conflicting demands within the family, or just because they have simply reached the 'end of the road' and can go no further.

It is this third reason which is usually the precursor to the search for suitable alternative residential care. Sue Davies and Mike Nolan (2003) found that there were five distinct areas of experience that carers had when faced with the task of finding a care-home:

- whether they felt themselves to be under pressure, or able to proceed with their search without a sense of urgency. Is this something that had been talked over and discussed with the person concerned (if possible) and with other people over a lengthy period, or had it been precipitated by some form of crisis?

- did the carers feel that they had sufficient knowledge about what they were looking for, what was available, what the alternatives were and which were the more appropriate; or were they basically working in the dark?

- were they working together or working apart? Was this a line of action that they were agreed upon, or was one member of the family pressing ahead with the silent or voiced opposition of other members of the family? There is a common scenario where the daughter-in-law takes the major responsibility for caring whilst the son is out at work and does not see or feel the full burden of care. Or where the spouse runs out of steam and the children, who may live far away, may not see why the action has been taken

- is it a process that the carer feels in control of, or do they feel themselves to be carried along by some 'external force' that they can neither identify nor control? And finally,

- do they feel that they are being supported throughout this process, and after the decisions have been taken; or do they feel very unsupported and therefore possibly, have feelings of guilt and anger that are not shared nor worked through with someone? Davies and Nolan comment:

> many carers were therefore left to make the decision alone, with little chance to discuss the emotional impact on themselves . . . in the few cases when relatives did receive continued support from a person who appreciated their needs, it was perceived as enormously helpful.

This is clearly an area where local churches could, if sensitive enough, provide support, information, and an ongoing forum for discussion and practical help. A further problem for many elderly carers who see their partner going into care, is whether they have the means to be able to visit them on a regular basis. Again, this is another area where local churches can make a contribution.

Margaret Jeremiah (2003) wrote that she had no idea what to look for in choosing a Residential Home, but with help from her family she drew up a short list of five which they then visited. Eventually they chose one which seemed to fit their needs most nearly and in many ways it did but, she writes:

> .. nothing in this life is perfect. On the downside we found later that nearly all the staff were untrained girls and boys from the village, spectacles and hearing aids got mixed up and as it was almost impossible to sort them out they were never worn….. I was never given satisfactory reason as to why none of the rooms, even the toilets, had any means of identification. The night staff were expected to get

everybody up and ready for breakfast by 7am so there was little time to be patient with people who did not feel co-operative at that time in the morning, or had strong views about what they would wear. They were therefore bundled into whatever was available and easiest to get on. Incontinence, not helped by the difficulty of finding the lavatory, necessitated frequent laundering of clothes, which sometimes were not available on time or no longer fitted.

In Scotland, a new watchdog for Care Homes (nursing homes and residential homes) was established in April 2002 and in its first Annual Report published in January 2004 it revealed that almost one complaint for every five care homes was upheld. Among the problems investigated were – residents not getting enough to eat, being dressed in other people's clothes and in one instance wearing someone else's false teeth. Standards in nursing homes seemed to be causing greater concern than in residential homes, with three times the number of complaints. A spokesperson for Help the Aged in Scotland said: "Every time we hear these stories, we are appalled that people are not being treated with the dignity that we expect to be afforded in our old age. It is dreadful".[21] What this illustrates is that there are real problems and anxieties to be addressed when thinking of this sort of residential care. On the other hand, these figures suggest that the vast majority of homes did not have complaints made against them, and so people should be able to proceed with a fair degree of expectation that a suitable home might be found. It is a process that cries out for sensitive pastoral support.

Drugs

There are three main areas where drugs may be used for people with dementia. There are those which aim to prevent or modify the development of the underlying pathology of the illness. There are those which may be used to address health issues which may be running parallel to the person's dementia – depression, for instance. Thirdly, there are those which are used to control or

---

[21] As reported in *The Herald* January 9th 2004

modify behaviour. Each has its own specific place in a person's care. But they can present the prescribing doctor with a number of problems:

- inadequate knowledge of the drug – this is a relatively new area and new drugs are constantly being brought onto the market, none of which have a long proven case-record for the doctor to fall back on

- uncertainty about the appropriateness of a particular drug for a particular person

- unreal expectations and hopes of the family, especially in the light of occasional graphic headlines in the newspapers suggesting that a new cure has just been found

We now know that there are a number of drugs which are of proven clinical benefit, others that have possible, but as yet unproven benefit and a large number that have no or extremely doubtful benefit. Tony Bayer (2001) discusses these in a very accessible way in his article in the periodical *Signpost,* and concludes that: 'the result of recent research gives considerable cause for optimism'.

Although the situation is improving, there still tends to be something of a post-code lottery as far as new drugs are concerned, and carers need to be vigilant in this area and be prepared to fight their corner if necessary.

A few words of caution

If relationships between people are not very good, then it is unlikely that the experience of dementia will strengthen them. We have to recognise the fact that there are many families where there are enormous stresses and fractures between the generations, sometimes for very good reasons. Similarly not every marriage is one of mutual love, care and consideration. Many marriages hang together by the skin of their teeth and for them, a diagnosis of dementia can be the final straw. We are already aware of how difficult it is to care for someone whom you love, so imagine the dynamics when there is little or no love between the people, and yet one of them is cast into the role of carer. Quite a lot of people use the words 'loved one' when speaking or writing about people with dementia but personally I would urge caution unless we actually know that the relationship is one of love and not of a grudging sense of obligation.

What are the obligations of family membership?

A wider issue is that of questioning what is the responsibility of family members to provide care for people as they grow older or become ill (Pitkeathley 1989):

> The ethical responsibility of people towards those who are close to them, particularly to parents, should be seen as a matter of choice and not as an obligation. This is a difficult concept for many people to accept, especially for those who have been brought up within a moral environment which has stressed the commandment to 'honour thy father and mother' without exploring what this might mean or reflecting upon the moral ambiguities that it might create. (Goldsmith 1999)

What, if any, are the obligations of family members towards other members of the family who suffer from dementia? This may seem a straightforward question, but it is one fraught with difficulties and to address it can open up a can of worms! Many daughters and daughters in law are placed in situations of enormous ambiguity, where they have to balance the demands made upon them by their own children, their partner, their elderly relatives (their own or their partners) and also take a care for their own needs. It can be a cause of enormous stress and tension.

Do grown children owe their parents something for all the care and nurture that they received as children? A growing number of people are now saying 'No' to that question. English (1979) argues that children did not ask to be brought into the world, it was their parents who chose to have them and therefore any ongoing relationship must only be on the basis of genuine friendship and love, and not at all through any sense of obligation. She writes "when friendship is absent the demands of reciprocity are absent as well . . . filial obligation or debt can serve as a maleficent ideological warrant for the destruction of daughters". Strong words, but ones which will strike a chord with many daughters or daughters in law. Sommers (1986) follows a similar line of argument but differs from English in developing the concept of gratitude.

According to Sommers gratitude is a response on the part of those who have received, to the generosity of those who have given. It is different to obligation, which is 'placed' upon people. Gratitude springs from the receiver. So in the context of dementia care, the task of caring should be seen as a matter of choice and not of obligation. This is a really complex area, and so much will depend upon the nature and the quality of people's relationships over a large number of years. The onset of dementia turns neither the person with the illness nor their family into some sort of superhuman person or people overnight, if at all.

It therefore comes as little surprise to discover that there is usually a considerable amount of guilt floating around in any household or family where there is a person with dementia. There is a difference, of course, between *feeling* guilty and *being* guilty. Many people feel guilty because they think that they have failed to live up to the standards of care that they set themselves or that they think other people expect from them (Woods 1997). Jane Crisp (2000) warns against this vicious spiral:

> If we begin by setting an impossible standard for ourselves, refusing all help and trying to be there for them all day, every day, we will end up exhausting ourselves . . . In an ideal

world, and with unlimited money and energy, we could probably have done more for my mother than we did. But by learning to accept the limits of what we could manage to do, both of us were able to last the distance and to keep in touch with her regardless of occasional setbacks and bad days, right to the end.

This chapter began by quoting a rather bleak scenario for the carer. It told the truth, but not the whole truth. A rather different perspective is offered by Ford (2003) who writes:

Virtually unseen by politicians and the public, men and women who are caregivers often sacrifice not only income, but time, jobs, career opportunities, individual interests and, sometimes, their own mental health to carry out what they accept as a personal responsibility. Such costly acts of mercy can also bring rewards, including a sense of closure, social approval, and especially, true personal and spiritual satisfaction.

This view is endorsed by Maureen Russell (Russell 2001) who embarked upon her task as a carer, gradually seeing it as the basis for spiritual development and formation. Hers is not a usual approach or experience, but it is an authentic one and needs to be noted:

Listening to the experience of dementia from a theological perspective, there is a paradox; in spite of everything to the contrary, I believe that my experience caring for someone with dementia has given me a sense of hope, because of an awareness of the wider horizon of a faith perspective. One who knows the despair of dementia and reaches out to another finds a sense of God's transcendent love. I think this love comes into sharper focus when we acknowledge each another's pain. The profound work of the Spirit searches our dark places and we can recognise new possibilities against the horizon of the infinite.

Not everyone is able or prepared to make the sacrifice entailed in caring, for a whole variety of reasons. One of the things that I have learned in my own pastoral ministry is to endeavour not to make judgements on the ways in which people try to cope with the pressures of their lives. It is easy to apportion blame to those whose full story we shall never know. If people decide that they will act in ways which might not be what we personally expected (assuming that everything is legal and there is no abuse of any kind), then we must allow them to act as they think best, without making any moral judgement. We can never be fully aware of the struggles and tensions that carers experience and there may be times when we are asked to stand alongside them as they seek to live with the decisions that they make, for better or for worse.

A plea from the heart

When you feel that not only does no one understand but you get the feeling (rightly or wrongly) that friends and relations and even one's own church do not want to understand or even know about what you are both experiencing it makes for a very rough and weary road to follow. You have no previous experience to fall back on and no lights at the end of the tunnel. (Jeremiah 2003)

So how can our churches help?

That will be the substance of the remainder of this book.

Lord, you will understand the grief of Mary
    as she watched your pain and sadness
    as your life drained away.
Be close to all who watch as
    illness relentlessly saps the vitality and life
    from those for whom they care.
In those shared experiences of caring and being cared for,
    may there be also
        the shared experiences of your presence
        and your promises of peace.

PART THREE
THE RESPONSE OF THE LOCAL CHURCH

Dare I name it a fellowship of the foolish? For foolish we most certainly will appear in a society obsessed by the quantifiable, by the immediate, by productivity and usefulness, by competition and profit, by individualism and loss of community and where the bottom line really is the bottom line. In that world it is accounted madness to expend precious resources on those who in economic terms are useless. There is, however, another larger world represented by a foolish, passionately extravagant woman pouring her alabaster jar of costly, perfumed oil over the head and feet of a man named Jesus – Tama a te Atua – Son of God. This kind of costly, extravagant care bears within it a power to heal our own human woundedness. In our hearts we know it, but we need each other's courage and a certain authentic and holy innocence for such foolishness.[22]

Eileen Shamy

---

[22] From the Introduction to her book *A Guide to the Spiritual Dimension of Care for People with Alzheimer's Disease and Related Dementia,* 2003

Chapter 8

Questions that are Frequently Asked

I suppose it is only natural, when we are confronted by a crisis in our life, that we are forced into a process of reflection and questioning. When that crisis involves suffering and possibly the prospect of the end of life as we know it, then the questioning becomes more fundamental and the reflection more time consuming. When a diagnosis of dementia is given, there has usually been a time – perhaps of several years – when questions have been raised, though not necessarily shared. Usually, by the time that the diagnosis has been given and shared, the person with dementia and probably their family or friends have quite a number of questions, about the nature of the illness and about the impact that it is likely to have upon their lives. Hopefully the doctor giving the diagnosis will have begun to talk through these and will have given people some written material and pointed them in the direction of continuing help, by suggesting contact with the local Alzheimer's Association or similar group.

People should never be afraid of asking questions, nor worry if they cannot always remember or understand the answers that are offered to them. Asking questions and receiving information is quite a complex process and, in general terms, we can only take on board so much new material at any one time. Although a person may have asked the same question last week, he or she may not have been in the right frame of mind to receive the answer or explanation, so it is quite appropriate that it be raised again. Questions and answers involve a two-way process and both the questioner and the person being questioned have a responsibility to try and make themselves understood. Sometimes it is quite difficult actually to frame a question, to put into words precisely what it is that is niggling away at the back of a person's mind. Similarly, it is not always easy to understand what the questioner is really saying, nor is it necessarily easy to couch an answer in words and images that the questioner might be able to receive and understand. Sometimes the questions are difficult to answer without first discussing the wider context – such as those questions identified by Bender and Cheston (1997): What will happen to me? Will I end up in a dementia ward? Will I become incontinent? Will my husband/wife stay with me or will they have me put away? These are the big 'global fears' that may surface immediately before more detailed and specific issues come to mind.

There are additional complications when the person who is asking the questions is also the person who has dementia. Are they able to remember what it is that they want to ask? Have they used the appropriate words? Can they remember what is being spoken back to them? It is a good idea therefore for people to jot down on a piece of paper the questions that they want to raise, and it is helpful if spoken answers can be backed up by the written word. It is not always possible, of course. There are no absolute rules, we are dealing with an art-form rather than with scientific method. However difficult the process may be, people have a fundamental right to know about their condition and to have their questions answered as fully and honestly as possible in ways that they can understand and assimilate.

Many of the questions that people want answered understandably relate to the physical, medical nature of their condition. But there are other, 'existential' questions that are also frequently asked, and several of these may well be of a religious nature. If people are to minister effectively and appropriately, from a Christian perspective, to people with dementia then they will need to have given some thought to the sort of questions which might well be asked of them.

What has brought this about; is it a punishment from God?

The causes of dementia are not yet fully understood. We now have a much clearer (though still incomplete) understanding of what is happening within the brain, and we know quite a lot about its chemical and electrical impulses. However, we are still a long way from being able to state with any certainty that dementia is caused by a specific action or influence. We do not have a correlation such as exists between smoking and lung cancer. We know, however, that certain other conditions may make dementia more likely – Parkinson's disease, AIDS or Down's syndrome, for example. But we are not able to state clearly and categorically how or why a person's dementia has been caused. All these plaques and tangles, what causes them? Is it something in the genes, or in upbringing or in the environment? We just do not know.

If the jury is still out in terms of explaining the physical causes of dementia, it is definitely not out when it comes to asking whether this is in some way a punishment from God. Most certainly and emphatically it is not. A god who hands out illness and suffering, pain and distress is not God as understood and experienced within the Judaeo-Christian tradition. Such capriciousness belongs more to the 'god' Setebos in *The Tempest* who was the subject of the musing of Caleban in Browning's poem. In that poem he envisages Setebos acting as he does and deciding who or what to punish in a most bizarre and arbitrary manner. He sees a number of crabs passing by:

> let twenty pass, and stone the twenty first,
> Loving not, hating not, just choosing so.
> Say, the first straggler that boasts purple spots
> Shall join the file, one pincer twisted off;
> Say, this bruised fellow shall receive a worm,
> And two worms he whose nippers end in red;
> As it likes me each time, I do: so He

The God of Christian tradition does not act so. God does not single people out in such a way and then punish them. No doubt when people look into themselves and reflect upon their lives, amongst so much that is wholesome and positive there may also be some things they regret or of which they are ashamed. Tasks not done as well as they might have been, unkind words here and ungenerous acts there. Sins of omission and commission. At times of crisis or illness it is perhaps understandable that people reflect on and remember these, but whatever they may or may not have done, God does not intervene in this way and inflict suffering and punishment on them. That is entirely out of keeping with the belief that we are here by the grace of God to enjoy and fulfil the life that has been given to us.

There is a strand within Christian tradition which sees God as the one who ultimately judges and rewards or punishes us according to our deeds. Mercifully it is not the only strand. But even within that frame of reference, punishment is delayed until after death and would not be seen as encompassing a person's health here and now.

There are many people in our churches who too readily adopt judgmental and punitive attitudes. Such people may well be susceptible to lines of thought which suggest that people 'get their due' and that there could well be some correlation between past activities and present suffering. Perhaps our churches tend to attract such people. It is part of the paradox of recognising that churches are made up of fallible and not-yet-fully-whole people, which is all of us, whilst at the same time wanting to be centres of compassionate understanding in a complex and pained society. Such judgmental people would tend to resist the approach to dementia that is being argued in this book. They would be firm supporters of what might now be called the 'old' culture of dementia care, which sadly is still the most prevalent approach in our society, but this is not to say that all those in the 'old' culture are necessarily judgemental!

But to return to the main thrust of this section. Mainstream Christian thought would want to recognise that we live within a broken world, and within an imperfect society, and that it is within this world and within this society that we are encouraged to live as creatively and as lovingly as we are able. God's will for us is for health and happiness, for the fulfilment of our potential and for unity with one another and with the One who is both our source and our ultimate destiny. Never, ever, does God intervene and punish us by inflicting illness or disease, suffering or tragedy upon us. Some people may need a great deal of reassurance as they struggle with their feelings and their questions. Trying to make sense of feelings of free-floating guilt (for whatever reason), coming to terms with this illness and thinking about the ultimate mystery (which may be perceived in the most primitive of images), will almost certainly occupy the minds of people with dementia and their carers. There is a job of real compassionate and sensitive pastoral support that may be called for in such a situation, a task that may require a great deal of patient listening without attempting to provide 'answers'.

If this condition is not a punishment from God, then what is it? It is yet another example of how the immense complexity and wonder of human life and the mechanism of our minds and bodies occasionally develop in what appear to be aberrant ways. We do not yet know why the intricate genetic patterns of our bodies always behave in the way that they do. In time I am sure that we shall understand a great deal more about why they react in one way rather than another in the whole area of dementia, but for the moment we have to live with what appears to be a largely random and unaccountable distribution of suffering. Part of the cost of being human is the fact that we have to live in a world in which there is so much that we do not understand – but it is also part of the thrill and fascination of being human. Being alive is itself a risky business, we all know that.

Why should this happen to me?

The broadcaster Gerald Priestland said of Rabbi Harold Kushner's book *When bad things happen to good people* (1981) that "so far as there is an answer to the conflict between the goodness of God and the bitterness of suffering, this is it". Kushner's son Aaron died when he was just fourteen years old, and this book was written to try and grapple with the question 'Why should this happen to me?' – or to my family, or to someone I love. It is a question which is frequently asked in the context of dementia care.[23]

In a very readable and accessible style, Kushner reflects at length on the story of Job and grapples with some of the painful pastoral situations he has been presented with as a Rabbi. He is honest about the tension that is sometimes felt when people who clearly are good people, endeavouring to live lovingly and creatively meet up with tragedy, illness and pain. So often those whom we perceive to be righteous seem to suffer and those whom we identify as unrighteous seem to prosper. This is an age old problem and certainly one which tormented the writers of some of the Psalms. But the Bible gives us an ambiguous and sometimes contradictory slant on these things. We have to come to terms with verses such as Proverbs 12v21 "No harm befalls the righteous, but the wicked have their fill of trouble" and Job 4v7 "Who, being innocent, has ever perished? Where were the upright ever destroyed?" The only way round such verses, which clearly do not match up with our own experience and observation of life, is to say that there is no such thing as a righteous person – in which case the whole discussion seems rather pointless.

When we ask the question "why should this happen to me?" we are not really expecting an answer, for we know that the question ultimately has no answer. If God does not dole out pain and suffering to one person and health and prosperity to another, then the thought that there must be a (moral) reason why this person

---

[23] See also *Where is God when it hurts* by Philip Yancy

suffers from Alzheimer's disease rather than their neighbour clearly doesn't stand up to scrutiny. There may be neurological reasons, there may be chemical and biological reasons why one person gets Alzheimer's and another has a stroke, whilst someone else suffers from cancer, but there are no moral reasons. It has nothing to do with how loving or forgiving or generous or clever or interesting a person may or may not have been. We know that sickness is no respecter of persons, and yet it seems inevitable that we continue to ask the question. And the reason why the question is still asked so often is because ultimately it is not so much a search for knowledge as a cry of pain. It is not that the intellect needs to be satisfied but rather that the person needs to be loved and accepted, affirmed and cherished. They need to be reassured that this is in no way some form of punishment or retribution for what they may or may not have done or been. Kushner writes:

> Laws of nature do not make exceptions for nice people. A bullet has no conscience; neither does a malignant tumour or an automobile gone out of control. That is why good people get sick and get hurt as much as anyone . . . God does not reach down to interrupt the workings of laws of nature to protect the righteous from harm . . . and really, how could we live in this world if He did . . . would this be a better world, if certain people were immune to laws of nature because God favoured them, while the rest of us had to fend for ourselves?

The question to be asked is not "Why has this happened to me?" because there is no answer to that, but rather "How am I going to cope with this? What resources do I have and where can I find help and support?" These are the questions which can open up constructive dialogue, which can pave the way for spiritual growth and open up issues about the very nature of God. It has often been said that God does not take away our problems, our pains and our sufferings but offers us a way through them, not by exerting some supernatural power but by sharing the agonies that we experience. I came across these two verses from Lee Webber (1994). They contain insights which are of value to people with dementia and also to those who are engaged in ministering to them:

I came to the swift, raging river
And the roar held the echo of fear,
'O Lord, give me wings to fly over
If You are, as You promised, quite near".

But he said "Trust the grace I am giving
All-pervasive, sufficient for you.
Take my hand – we will face this together
But my plan is – not over, but through".

John Austin Baker was a theologian bishop and he surprised many people by writing a slim novel *Travels in Oudamovia (1976)* which tried to address some of the problems associated with suffering. He wrote:

There is only one way in which, with the world as it is, God can show himself good in respect of man's suffering; and that is by not asking of us anything that he is not prepared to endure himself. He must share the dirt and the sweat, the bafflement and the loneliness, the pain, the weakness, yes, and the death too. That would be a God one could respect, a God who put aside all his magic weapons, and did it all as one of us. A God who, when we cry out in misery (as we all do), 'Why should this happen to me?' can answer truthfully, 'It happened to me too . . .'

What will happen to my faith?

Given what we know about the nature of dementia, it is not surprising that many people wonder what will happen to their faith if they journey down this road of forgetfulness. It is a difficult question to answer as everyone is different, and the ways in which people experience and express their faith is also different. Robert Davis for instance, in his book (1987) reflected on ". . .the cruellist blow of all. This personal and tender relationship that I had with the Lord was no longer there". Christine Boden, on the other hand can write (1998) "My book is not a miserable story. I am happy and very much at peace with what is happening to me . . . without my faith in God, I would not have been able to cope with this devastating illness".

In a later book (2002) Christine Bryden (formerly Boden, as above) contributed a chapter in which she wrote:

My journey along the path of dementia is one of survival with dignity. I refuse to be a victim, to succumb to the lie of dementia, that as my cognition fades, so too must my spirituality. I will trust in the Holy Spirit within me, and the fellowship of the body of Christ around me, to help me as I make this journey. My soul remains my mainstay, as I travel this path of making meaning in life, and of discovering the glory of God within me.

Most people however do not write books, nor are they necessarily good at conceptualising and analysing how they feel and how they understand the progression of their illness. So it is left to others to try and gauge how they are coping in terms of their faith, and here again, most people are not accustomed to thinking in those sorts of terms, certainly not in the British tradition anyway! It would seem that people with dementia, if they are accustomed to going to church, like to continue that habit; it provides a context of stability and predictability, and a community within which they can feel safe. It is a great help if they have a partner who accompanies them and for whom this also is a time of acceptance and calmness. It is more difficult if the person with dementia lives alone, and if that is the case then the local congregation can make a point of sitting by them, supporting them, noticing if they are absent and perhaps the following week reminding them about the service an hour or so before it begins. When people live with other family members who are not accustomed to going to church, then they may feel that they are imposing an additional burden by asking to go, and in these situations the habit of church attendance can come to an end. Local churches need to be sensitive and alert to these situations and offer help, support and transport whenever it is needed.

For some people, as their illness progresses, attendance at services can be problematic. Problematic for the person concerned, problematic for their partner or family member and problematic for the congregation. There may be moments of erratic behaviour, suddenly singing in a quiet part of the service, speaking quite loudly or needing to move about. Knowing that this is a possibility and recognising that this may be how dementia affects that particular person should enable congregations to develop sufficient skills and exercise sufficient tolerance and acceptance to enable the person to remain part of their worshipping community. This is part of their gift; but they are also receivers, for the life and authenticity of the congregation is enormously enriched by holding within it people who are not cognitively and behaviourally "normal". The newsletter of a group working with people with learning disabilities quoted the passage from 1 Corinthians (12v22) – "those parts of the body that seem to be weaker are indispensable" and it went on to say "this verse says that such people are indispensable, we cannot do without them. I would go so far as to say that until a church is ready to welcome and integrate people with learning disabilities into its fellowship, it will be impoverished". The same can be said about people with dementia. Hughes (2003) puts it this way:

> . . .in the faces of people with dementia we should see our own fate and the fate of those we love. We should seek out the humanity of people with dementia in their remaining abilities. In so doing, we shall draw upon and reaffirm our own humanity and recognise our mutual dependency.

Some people may struggle with their faith when given a diagnosis of dementia because they feel that God must be punitive or unloving; they may feel that their years of church membership have failed to protect them from illness and loss or they may just have intellectual problems which they do not feel that they have the time or capacity to resolve. As with so many pastoral situations, it is impossible to be dogmatic. We cannot assure people that their faith will continue to be the important feature in their life that it may have been in earlier times, but nor can we assume that the journey into dementia will destroy a person's faith or make it irrelevant. Furthermore, there are many examples of people discovering and delighting in faith as they come to terms with their illness.

In reality, though, the important question is not so much 'what will happen to my faith in God?' as 'what will happen to God's faith in me?'. To that question there can be an unequivocal answer. God's faith in and love for people with dementia remains constant, irrespective of whether their illness robs them of remembrance of God or not. And this is surely the good news of the Gospel. Faith does not depend upon our love for God but upon God's love for us. As the American nun Sister Laura remarked to David Snowdon (2001) reflecting on her diagnosis of Alzheimer's disease:

> "Dr.Snowdon, do you know what my worst fear was?" Now her eyes started to well up with tears. "That I was going to forget Jesus," she said. "I finally realised that I may not remember Him, but He will remember me."

What about the Faith of the caregivers?

Carers will have many of the same questions to ask, and the answers will be similar. But there is one extra question that they will probably be wrestling with, and that is, how will they maintain sufficient strength, patience, hope and faith to allow them to continue as caregivers. The week that I write this I have been following the story in the newspapers of a church elder, married to his wife for over sixty years, who could bear it no longer and placed a pillow over his wife's face and smothered her. He had seen his gentle wife become aggressive, abusive and an apparent stranger to him. His years of caring had placed a burden upon him that he could no longer tolerate, and so for his own sake and also for his wife's, he brought them to an end.

Carers within a community of faith should look to that community for help and support, and ask for the particular things which might make life more tolerable. Outsiders, looking on, often feel very helpless and unsure of what they should do or what they can offer. In an ideal world people would have such imaginative compassion that there would be no need to ask, but for most of us there is still a great invisible wall between our needs and the possible sources of support and encouragement. It is also important for carers to continue to remain in touch with their church, and to find ways in which they can recharge the batteries or find a moment or two of solitude for reflection. Getting tired, feeling depressed, losing hope or becoming irritable or angry are not things to be ashamed of. They are some of the natural consequences of caring. They can be addressed by finding refreshment and stimulation for themselves – that is not being selfish or uncaring – it is being realistic and it is being practical, and it will ultimately improve their capacity to care.

In terms of religious faith, the carer often has to "have faith for both of us", or so it may seem. That is part of what it means to belong to each other and to belong to a community of faith. But others also within the congregation should be encouraged to share in this 'burden of believing'. 'Burden' not in the sense of being weighed down and overwhelmed, but 'burden' in the sense of sharing a responsibility, being part of a community, in much the same way as parents will bring their children within the orbit and influence of the worshipping community; they do it on behalf of their children. 'Bear ye one another's burdens' (Galatians 6 v2).

It is important that the carer has places in which they can be honest, in which they can cry or shout, be angry or be silent. It is also important that they find people with whom they can talk and share things, without feeling guilty or unfaithful. It is a difficult journey that the carer is having to tread. It may not be as dramatic or as awful as the one facing the person with dementia, but it should not be dismissed nor its pain and difficulties under-estimated. Hopefully there will be occasional times of grace; times for feeling gratitude or experiencing loving acceptance and encouragement. There will also be possibilities for spiritual reflection and growth, an awareness that God's ways are not our ways, nor ours God's. I don't write this with a hidden agenda of trying to suggest that God wishes people to suffer in order that they, or we, may grow in grace. I don't believe that. But I do believe that often situations of pain and weariness may, in some strange way, make us more receptive to other ways of looking at things, other ways of thinking through our priorities and recognising the value and meaning of many things (or people) which hitherto we may often have taken for granted.

Take, for instance this reflection written by a daughter about her mother. It expresses much of the sorrow and sadness that she feels and is realistic about the losses that are experienced, and yet there is also a sense of resigned hope and a sense of sad peace which, strangely enough, are quite healing.

> Slowly slipping away
> Like grains of sand through my fingers
> One day laughing
> One day crying
> Never knowing how much I love her
> Or how sad I feel about who she has become
> So I cry
> I cry because she will never hear her grandson's laughter
> And I know that he is part of her
> So I weep
> I weep because she will never see her baby, my brother
> Getting married, raising a family
> Even if she sees, she will never understand
> So I sob
> I sob big, racking sobs
> Because her life is gone and ours must continue
> But one day
> There is laughter at a joke, understood
> So I smile
> I smile because for one moment she is back
> Back in our world, among us

So I am happy
I am happy because life's huge problems
    do not weigh on her mind
So I am glad
I am glad that little things like a flower
    or a bird
      will still light up her face
So I am content
I am content because I see God's huge arms
Enveloping her
Embracing her
And welcoming her into His world
A world of peace
Where all is understood
And all is beautiful
So I sigh[24]

Questions questions questions
Lord there are so many questions
    and so few answers.
And yet, within this crazy, frenzied situation
    where everything seems to be going wrong
There may be moments of peace
    and the emergence of an answer.
Not an answer to the questions that I ask
    but to the questions I don't ask.
      All will be well
      All will be well
      All will be ultimately well
I didn't know that
I didn't ask that
    and yet I dare to believe it

---

[24] *A Daughter* from *The Caregiver* Summer 1995. I have been unable to unearth any further information about this. If anyone can help, I will gladly acknowledge in any future editions.

Chapter 9

Spirituality and Dementia

All of a sudden, without most people becoming aware of it, spirituality has become the 'in' thing. Whereas a few years ago, the merest mention of the word would have been enough to turn people off or to trigger a change of subject for conversation, now it seems, spirituality is what life is all about and any self-respecting dementia carer needs to have a plan or a policy about it. In many ways I am delighted by this change in approach, this altered climate in which we now live, but the word 'spirituality' does seem to have the disadvantage of meaning just about anything. It is in danger of becoming whatever we want it to be. David Jenkins (2004) comments that he finds it "a weasel word used to obfuscate or avoid basic questions of reality".

Jeanne Lee (2003) describes the way in which her experience of dementia has led her to re-assess her life:

> I have become very spiritual of late, which I suppose is a natural tendency when one comes face to face with the end of life, or at least the end of life as one knows it. Alzheimer's has that kind of effect on a person, because life as I knew it is over, and what that life-changing circumstance has caused me to recognise is that I have two choices. The same two, I now realise, that I've always had; I can grow or shrivel; I can be happy or unhappy; I can dwell in the light or in the darkness; I can live in love or in fear. They are all really the same two choices, and the exciting thing to me is that the choice is always mine alone; always has been and always will be. And that choice is right now ... this moment. The choice we make in the moment creates our life. I now consider myself a spiritual person, or at least on the spiritual path, as opposed to

> a religious person . . . . slowly, slowly my old way of
> thinking is being replaced by the new and better way.

She sees herself as a spiritual person 'as opposed to a religious person'. At a time when organised religion is going through something of a crisis in terms of membership, there is blossoming, and being acknowledged, a whole new area of experience loosely called 'spiritual'. "Everyone is spiritual but not everyone is religious" seems to be the general way of expressing it. A speaker at one conference I attended had an interesting slant on the subject when he said "I want a spirituality for life without God and a hereafter first. Then, and only then, will I seek a spirituality with God and the hereafter". In recent years there have been a number of studies exploring spirituality and health issues, which include the relationship between spirituality and dementia. From these it is possible to extract a whole range of definitions about what the writers believe spirituality is all about.

Julia Barton et al (2003) introduce their understanding of spirituality with a little story. Imagine a university lecturer holding up a pristine £20 note and asking who would like it. Every hand would go up. The lecturer then folds the note and generally creases it up and asks the same question to the class. Every hand again goes up. The note is now place on the floor and walked over, so that it eventually emerges as crumpled and dirty. Again the lecturer asks who would like it, and again every hand goes up; the note does not lose its value, value is not dependent upon condition:

> Likewise, human beings, though dropped, crumpled and stepped on during the course of their lives, never lose value. Their worth is determined by who they are more than by what they have done. This intrinsic value and worth is a large part of how we define spirituality.

One of the best definitions that I have come across is contained in a small booklet *Frequently asked questions on Spirituality and Religion* by Jo Airey and others (2002). They write:

It is common for the words religion and spirituality to be used interchangeably. This tendency both narrows the scope of the latter and also fails to acknowledge the non-material aspects of life enjoyed by those without a particular faith. Religion can be seen as a framework that some people use to make sense of the world and their place within it. Religion provides a set of beliefs to adhere to and guidelines to follow. It offers an explanation for a sense of being at one or of wholeness in relation to God. Spirituality is the experience of the raw feelings – the moments of joy, bewilderment, hope, awe, understanding and wonder – that we all experience at various points of our lives. These can be interpreted within or without a religious framework. Spirituality is the energy of a lived life. Religion is a community-shared story.

There have been many other attempts to try and explain just what is meant by these terms. The list below is taken from Aldridge (2000), MacKinlay (2002) and elsewhere. Although acknowledging authorship of the quotations, I have not referred to the books in question and if you want to explore them further I would refer you back to David Aldridge and Elizabeth McKinlay's books. This is only a selection of the definitions to be found there.

- Spirituality is a belief system focusing on intangible elements that impart vitality and meaning to life events (*Joseph*)

- Spirituality is ... the experiential integration of one's life in terms of one's ultimate values and meanings (*Muldoon & King*)

- Spiritual ... means in essence 'searching for existential meaning'. Spiritual beliefs may be expressed in religion and its hallowed practices, but a person can and often does have a spiritual dimension to his or her life that is totally unrelated to religion and not expressed or explored in religious practice (*Doyle*)

- Not only of belief in God but of a relationship with a supreme power, often a relationship that includes prayer in some form. Others speak of the conviction that life has a purpose, of the search for meaning, of the attempt to interpret their present illness in a way that makes sense within their world-view (*Smyth & Bellemare*)

- Definitions of spirituality ... referred to a dynamic, principle, or an aspect of a person that related to God or god, other persons, or aspects of personal being or material nature ... the spiritual dimension was used to refer to a quality beyond religious affiliation that is used to inspire or harmonize answers to questions regarding infinite subjects e.g., meaning and purpose of life and one's relation to the universe (*Emblen*)

- Six clear factors .... appear to be fundamental aspects of spirituality ... those of the journey, transcendence, community, religion, 'the mystery of creation' and transformation (*Lapierre*)

- Spirituality .... pertains to one's relationship with others, with oneself and with one's higher power, which is defined by the individual and need not be associated with a formal religion *(Borman & Dixon)*

- Spirituality is rooted in an awareness which is part of the biological make-up of the human species. Spirituality is present in all individuals and it may manifest as an inner peace and strength derived from perceived relationship with a transcendent God or an ultimate reality or whatever an individual values as supreme (*Narayanasamy*)

- That which lies at the core of each person's being, an essential dimension which brings meaning to life. Constituted not only by religious practices, but understood more broadly, as relationship with God, however God or ultimate meaning is perceived by the person, and in relationship with other people *(MacKinlay)*

- Spiritual elements are those capacities that enable a human being to rise above or transcend any experience at hand. They are characterized by the capacity to seek meaning and purpose, to have faith, to love, to forgive, to pray, to meditate, to worship, and to seek beyond present circumstances *(Kuhn)*

- A state where an individual shows by their life example and attitudes, a sense of peace with themselves and others, and development of wholeness of being. The search for meaning and a degree of transcendence is evident *(MacKinlay)*

With such a plethora of approaches to and understanding of what is meant by the term "spirituality" it is not difficult to have a certain degree of sympathy with David Jenkins when he says that it has become a "substitute for 'faith' and is rapidly shrunk to be, in effect, 'religiosity', something to be indulged in according to personal and individual taste". This is a point of view taken up by Jonathan Sacks (2002) the Chief Rabbi, when he writes:

Spirituality good, religion bad. That seems to be the current state of the Western soul. Church attendance is down, but interest in the soul, the self, the intimate geography of the mind, is alive and well . . . . which must be good news mustn't it? It shows that we are not just materialists, hedonists, and consumers undergoing retail therapy. We have a soul. We care. We meditate. We commune. We are in touch with higher worlds. We are, after all, children of the spirit in search of light. Well, yes, up to a point. But is spirituality really a substitute for religion . . . . there is much positive about our search for spirituality, but there is also something escapist, shallow and self-indulgent. Just as street protest is the attempt to achieve the results of politics without the hard work of politics, so the current cult of spirituality is the attempt to achieve the results of religion without the disciplines, codes and commitments of religion. That is not good news.

To discover God within the soul is easy. What is hard is to bring God into the world, with all its poverty, inequality, violence and terror, and make it a home for His presence by celebrating His image in others.

That takes real work, the long, hard, steady work of love in action, loyalty in deed, generosity to those who do not yet share your blessings. That's what makes pilgrims different from tourists, holy days different from holidays, and commitment something greater than the search for experience. Religion starts in spirituality. What it asks of us next is where the real work of God begins.

So there we have it; an acknowledgment of the universality of spirituality, but also a slight anxiety that it can overwhelm, suffocate or replace the discipline of faith. We need to find ways of exploring and affirming spirituality whilst recognising and acknowledging that there are differences as well as similarities between spirituality and faith. We do not commend faith by belittling spirituality. There is something very important about people's sense of sacredness, whether it be of time or space or revealed in other people. Rosemary Clarke (2003), in a moving little article explaining how she endeavoured (and in many ways succeeded) to find a 'way through' to her mother as she seemed to grow more and more incommunicative in her nursing home, says at the end – "I don't think it is an accident that I spend my time with my mother in these ways on my knees. Our time together is characterised by honesty, nothing in the way, by just being. It feels to be a sacred space".

Spirituality, religion and faith

Words can be confusing. Words relating to religion can be even more confusing, and words relating to religious experience can be the most confusing of all! But this is an important subject and one that requires us to tread with great sensitivity and compassionate imagination. I would hate to see a divide emerging between one set of people espousing spirituality and another pressing the claims of religion, each suspicious of the motives or the commitment of the other. The 'problem' of the looseness of language can be reinterpreted as an opportunity: an opportunity for new insights, new understanding and one which opens the door for creative, non-judgmental ministry.

The studies mentioned earlier are fascinating in the ways in which they cannot avoid recognising that there is something within men and women which hints at or speaks of, that which is beyond them. It seems as though the very nature of being human means that people have a need for something which transcends them and which can sustain, enthuse, comfort or sustain them. There may be many reasons for this, many different explanations. But we do not need to know the reasons why, to recognise that some things 'speak to our inner being' more than others do. Nor do we need to be precise about our language or our descriptive or analytical powers in order to experience this 'otherness'.

For some people, of course, it is important that they are precise and they fear being carried along by what they cannot understand or substantiate, and they may be particularly wary of 'feelings'. It is important that their approach and position is recognised and respected. Other people are less concerned about the detail and they want to explore and enjoy just what it is that seems to bring them peace or hope, meaning or strength. We are all different. But we are the same in that we gain greater satisfaction from some things, from some experiences, than we do from others.

In the realm of dementia care it is important that we endeavour to discover what it is that brings solace, satisfaction, hope or meaning to people, and then that we seek to find ways to ensure that they can continue to experience this, no matter how serious their condition. It is this 'spiritual dimension' which can be so important to all of us, and especially to people with dementia who may not be able to express their hopes and fears as clearly as they, or we, would wish.

Earlier (on page 95) I wrote about the importance of memory boxes. About placing a number of small objects, each of which has particular meaning and significance to a person, into a box so that they can be brought out, handled and become a focus for reflection or discussion, at a later time. There is a similar need to build up an understanding of what it is that might bring this sense of 'the other' to different people. It might be particular smells – I read of a man who hadn't spoken to anyone for many, many months suddenly remarking that the flowers that a visitor was carrying smelt just like his wife's bouquet on their wedding day sixty years earlier. People who have been keen gardeners might well need some of the smells, sounds or colours of the garden to feed their inner being. Music can be a magnificent friend – but only if you know the music that speaks to a particular person. A Rolling Stones fan might not appreciate something from The Sleeping Beauty; The Seekers may evoke all sorts of memories for another person, but not opera, whilst Beethoven's String Quartets might delight one person and be totally incomprehensible and torture to another.

Just what are the things that speak to a person's inner being, that encourage or sustain their sense of well-being? Part of imaginative and compassionate ministry is to discover these things. This nurturing of the 'spiritual' is an important part of ministry; it is not the complete task but it is certainly an essential part of it. Perhaps sitting with someone, maybe holding their hand, and listening to a tape of bird songs, or a piece of music, or glancing through a beautiful book may be doing more for a person's inner being than a multitude of prayers or a compendium of sermons! Robert Davis (1987) the minister admitted that he felt he was brought closer to God by the National Geographic magazine than by sermons.

This recognition of the importance of the spiritual side of life, which is increasingly being recognised by hospitals and nursing homes, gives the minister – who may be tentative and unsure of his or her ground, uncertain about the context and perhaps not knowing the person all that well – a wonderful opportunity to make contact. People are in need of, wanting, this sense of 'that which is beyond them'. They may not be wanting formal religion. They may not be wanting evangelism. They may not be wanting prayer or Bible reading, but almost everyone has a thirst and a need for their inner space to be recognised and honoured. The sensitive minister (be they lay or ordained) should have no fears about the importance of his or her role; but insensitivity can be a cruel and invasive liberty. Welcome this new openness to spirituality, loose and subjective though people's understanding of it might well be. But we need also to be humble as we approach the spirituality of another, for they may have much to teach us, and we may be moving into holy ground.

If the term 'spirituality' is all embracing, the scene can be narrowed down a little by looking at 'religion'. The word 'religion' points to ways in which humankind, over the centuries, has tried to understand, formulate, experience and communicate spiritual truths and insights. Not everyone who is spiritual is religious, but many are. Ideally, people who are religious are also spiritual, though sometimes we have to work hard to discover the roots of their spirituality. Religion involves some aspects of institutionalisation and institutions tend to have their own sets of rules and ways of doing things, their own rituals and their own ways of speaking, their own language or their own ways of understanding or interpreting words.

In simple terms, when dealing in the area of dementia care, we often want to know what 'religion a person is'. This can mean Jewish, Christian, Muslim, Sikh or any other religion – or none. In common parlance it often means where does that person 'sit' in relation to these great religious traditions. So often, in our culture, when we ask what religion a person is, we tend to assume Christianity and we are wondering whether they are a Catholic, a Baptist, a Methodist or a Scottish Episcopalian. Clearly, as our society becomes much more multi-cultural, there will be many more people from the great religions of the world entering into our residential and nursing homes and into our hospitals.

Within the context of this book we are wanting to be able to assess if the person with dementia would regard themselves as a Christian or not. If they are not, then we may well wish to pass them onto the spiritual leaders of their own particular faith. A helpful booklet *Religious Practice and People with Dementia*[25] was published in 2002 by the Christian Council on Ageing. Some people, of course, belong to no particular faith community, nor would they wish to, and their perspective on these things should be honoured and respected. They may or may not welcome some form of compassionate ministry from the church.

It is helpful for us to know the religious background of people so that our approach to them can be as informed and as sensitive as possible. Some Christian traditions would expect a minister to pray with them and read the scriptures to them, other traditions might feel that this could be intrusive. Of course, all ministers will believe in the value of prayer and Bible reading, but just how and when to do this is a matter of judgement. As far as possible, the agenda should be set by the person with dementia and these things should not be imposed by other people. A minister is not 'failing' the person with dementia, themselves or God if they do not pray openly with a person. On the other hand this may be entirely appropriate. The important thing is that the minister is at ease with the person with dementia, and with their own style of ministry, and is not trying to hurry things along or impose things which are not wanted. Also, the person with dementia needs to be

---

[25] Obtainable from Christian Council on Ageing Dementia Project, Chaplaincy Centre, St Nicholas' Hospital, Jubilee Road, Gosforth, Newcastle upon Tyne NE3 3XT

at ease with the minister. It is a matter of balance and judgement. In my experience there is always time for silent prayer even when open prayer is not thought to be appropriate.

Knowing a person's religious background can also help us understand what their worship needs may be. I recall visiting a lady in a nursing home and discovering that she was a Roman Catholic who was in the habit of attending Mass daily. As far as I could ascertain, since her admission into the home she had never been to Mass nor had she been visited by a priest. Somewhere along the line this lady had been failed badly by those who were caring for her, whether in the home, in the community or in her church – I don't know, but her needs were not being met. For some people receiving the sacrament on a regular basis is of great importance, for other people they may not want that but would appreciate the continuance of some other aspect of their religious or worshipping life. Maybe a tape of hymns, or of readings. Perhaps attendance at a service or people from the church coming and holding a service where the person is now living. What is important to understand is the fact that because a person has dementia it does not mean that they are no longer in need or desirous of the rituals and practices of their religion.

If we have narrowed the broad term of spirituality down to religion, I would now like to narrow it down even further and speak of Faith. By that I am meaning, in the Christian context, someone who is committed to following Jesus. Other religions will have their own ways of expressing how a person has a living commitment to that religion, but for Christians this is expressed in terms of being a follower of Jesus. In narrowing the field down in this way I am not wanting to suggest that one is somehow more important or better than the other. I am, however, wanting to acknowledge that there are differences, and anyone who is engaged in ministry needs to be aware of them as they will affect the ways in which they will need to respond.

Perhaps this chapter needs to contain a few words of warning. Spirituality and religion, though in many ways wonderful and life enhancing, can also have a more problematic side. They are not a universal panacea, and they can be distorted, misunderstood, misinterpreted and misapplied. Not everyone's experience of religion has been wholesome and many people bear the scars of unenlightened or authoritarian religion.

When people develop dementia their short term memory is affected but their long term memory remains focused for a much longer time. They may forget the loving acceptance and support that they have received from their local church or community in recent years and they may remember incidents in their early life which gave a portrayal of an angry or unforgiving deity. Ministry today may pick up some of yesteryear's anger and hurt, just as in other cases, it picks up much of the value of yesteryear's work and nourishment.

People may turn to religion with unrealistic hopes and expectations and feel terribly hurt or disillusioned if their prayers are not answered in the way that they hoped. They may want instant results and 'success' and ministering in that context can be quite a demanding and daunting task. How to convey the story of God's love when people's experiences are of pain and despair has been a perennial task for the church over the centuries, and there is no easy answer to the questions raised. We have to live with the ambiguity and contradictions, we walk by faith rather than by certainty. It is not for nothing that the church has often been portrayed as a fragile sailing boat, perilously tossed about by the waves yet powered by the invisible wind of the Spirit in its sails.

Lord, you have placed us in a world full of mystery and beauty;
a world in which conflict and violence,
carelessness and pain so often hide your presence.
Help us to be sensitive to our inner being,
to recognise something of the awe of being human.
We give thanks for the religious traditions which seek to
communicate something of you and of your presence.
Help us to walk the way of faithfulness
whether we are in the light or in the shadows,
with alert minds or experiencing the depths of confusion.
May there always be those around us who can recognise
and cherish our innermost being;
Open our eyes and hearts
that we may recognise the same in others,
and in that sacred space, see something of you.

Chapter 10

Don't talk of love – Show me!

> In ageing we necessarily need to embrace both memory and hope without allowing either to dominate or detach us from the present. For it is always in the present moment with such resources as we possess that we are called upon to live as those made in God's image. (Kimble 2002)

This quotation from Mel Kimble, the Director of the Centre for Ageing, Religion and Spirituality in St Paul, Minnesota encapsulates the very essence of ministry. We take hold of the past, the history of the situation, we look towards the future with hope and confidence, but we do not let ourselves be bound by either. Then, with all the resources that God has given us for the moment, we engage with the work on hand.

The evening before I was ordained in 1962 I vividly remember the then Bishop of Birmingham, Leonard Wilson, in a devotional address to all the candidates saying that we would never be required to do any task without being given the resources to do it. This from a man who had been imprisoned and tortured by the Japanese following the invasion of Singapore where he was Bishop in 1942. After the war, taking a confirmation service in a prison he came face to face with one of the guards who was responsible for his torture. It seems likely that in the very process of being tortured he discovered resources that not only enabled him to survive, but also to influence profoundly the lives of people around him, although at the time he was conscious only of his suffering.

And so it is with the ministry of carers, and also, to a lesser degree, with our own ministries. We get on with the tasks that are presented to us each day. We hold together the past and the future, letting them both inform the present, and with compassion and sometimes with courage, we embark upon the work in hand. Our work alongside people with dementia is of this nature. It is not easy, we do not have 'answers' and we feel terribly vulnerable and inadequate, but that is the work that we have been called to do, and so with faith we embark upon it. Kerrie Hide (2002) says of this:

> caregivers who have an appreciation that being in the present moment in all our fragility and incompleteness is sacred, can enable people with dementia to experience glimpses of the divine.

Church attendance

Very often people with dementia drop out from our churches without being noticed. People who were regular worshippers may attend less frequently, they may become more reserved, they may begin to feel uneasy, feel that they are losing a grasp of what is happening and feel awkward in the presence of so many other people. So they gradually stop coming. It may take them much longer to get dressed or prepare for going out; they may forget what time it is or what time the service starts; they may forget what day it is. If they come with their family carers, they may occasionally embarrass them. Even within the church congregation they may embarrass other members who do not understand what is happening or how to respond appropriately. People who once did little jobs or contributed to the worship often find that they are being asked less often. In a thousand different ways our churches unwittingly send out signals that this is no place for the mentally confused. You have to have your wits about you if you are to cope with our liturgies, our different sheets of paper, our hymn books, prayer books and notices. Our standing up, sitting down and kneeling; our being quiet then singing then listening then speaking. Even churches which pride themselves on their services being 'straightforward' often do not recognise that they have their own rituals, their own way of doing things, their own way of 'being straightforward'. It is a very complex procedure and we need to ensure that we do everything possible to make our worship accessible to people, and this is particularly true if some of those people have dementia.

Not only must our worship be accessible, but also our community must be accessible. This means that our congregations need to be assisted to understand and embrace dementia. In my experience most congregations are made up of people who want to be good and who want to be kind and welcoming; but they are not always able to be so. They don't know how to handle people whom they deem to be different or difficult; they don't want to feel 'trapped' and so, very gradually, they find ways of avoiding them. It is a relatively simple task to encourage congregations to see their welcome of people as part of their own ministry. Congregations need to embrace the totality of human experience and they need to be places of welcome for 'all sorts and conditions of men'. But this usually needs some thought and preparation, some teaching and prayer. And of course, the thing about dementia is that the next person who develops it may be me – and what sort of community would I want around me, surely one of understanding, acceptance and support.

One study of dementia and spirituality reported a person's reflections in this way:

> I did stop going to church – the biggest reason – well there were two reasons – one of which I am not really enamoured of a God who creates something like Alzheimer's and the second is that I'm afraid of tripping

There may be a number of simple little things, like minimising the fear of tripping, that can help when people come to our churches. Are the toilets accessible and clearly labelled? Are the various books and papers given out to people with a friendly smile and welcome? Are people shown to a seat – not in a 'pushy' way, but quietly if it seems that the person coming through the door is a little confused. Are there people around who can help them find the hymns in the book if necessary? Are there people whose responsibility it is to ensure that strangers, or others, who appear to be finding things difficult are discreetly and encouragingly helped and supported. Someone who may have been a member of the church for many years may, with dementia, find the whole experience disconcerting and worrying. Are there jobs that people in the early stages of dementia are still able to do – take the collection, prepare the elements, gather up the books after the service. Remember, an important part of good dementia care is to focus upon the things that people are still able to do rather than on what they are no longer able to do. The early stages of dementia may last for quite a number of years and churches should be one of the communities that are able to provide support, understanding and engagement during this time.

There are also opportunities for church congregations to provide support and encouragement for those who care for people with dementia. Often they need a break, but are unable to leave the person at home without someone being there. Perhaps they need to be able to get to church by themselves sometimes, and to have time to be fed and nurtured themselves. Can people in the congregation provide some form of 'sitting-in' service. I know it is not always easy, but neither is it always hard.

Perhaps it would be a good idea if once a year each congregation underwent some form of audit to assess how dementia-friendly it was. It could reflect on where it could improve and how it could recognise and affirm the work that is going on and all the people who do, in so many ways help, encourage and support people in this situation. Let us not take fright at this, as Laraine Moffitt (1996) reminds us:

> While it is good to see 'meeting spiritual needs' given greater attention, we must beware of presenting this as a

sophisticated new skill – many care workers have always attended to spiritual needs, through individualised care. But there is also great benefit in helping people preserve or re-create a personal 'sacred space'

So there we have it – individualised care and the creation and maintenance of a personal sacred space – not a bad objective for our congregations to have in their ministry with and welcome of people with dementia.

Home visiting

Because people with dementia often don't remember who people are, and because it is sometimes difficult to have what we might think is a meaningful conversation with them, there is a great temptation for people to assume that it doesn't really matter whether they are visited or not. It is vitally important that we endeavour to keep in contact with them, that we continue to affirm who they are and work at ways in which we might be able to have a real meeting and a significant visit. The onus may be on the visitor to provide the stimulus and to keep the conversation going – though this is not always the case.

It is worthwhile therefore giving some thought to a visit before going. Is there any important news or information that you would like to share with them, have you anything to take with you – flowers, something to eat, or some photographs to talk about? Remember that people can meet together without exchanging words all the time, so don't feel that you have to fill every empty space with sound. Remember also that it takes much longer for people with dementia to process information, so take to heart some of the tips about communication that were discussed in Chapter 6. If a church congregation is being encouraged to share in this ministry it might be useful for them to have a copy of the little leaflet *Visiting people with dementia.*[26]

People with dementia often repeat the same stories or sentences over and over again and visitors can sometimes find this difficult to cope with, but the person will not be aware of the fact that they have told you it before. Occasionally they will say things which you feel are not true – they may say that some-one is trying to come into their room, for instance, or that someone comes in each day and takes their glasses – accept what they are saying and do not feel that you need to argue the case. It is not a matter of winning an argument. When you feel that you are on difficult ground, try to switch the subject of the conversation and talk about something else. Also try not to apportion blame to the person, they are not being 'difficult' on purpose, they are endeavouring to survive and live a normal life with a brain that is becoming increasingly damaged. The fact that you cannot see what is happening to their brain does not mean that nothing is happening. People are seldom just 'making things up' or deliberately being obstructive.

Sometimes it really is difficult to make much apparent headway; do not despair. There may be many reasons why some days are more difficult than others, it may be the effect of drugs, it may be that they have something else troubling them which you (and perhaps they) are not aware of. When the going gets tough, stay in there. Words are not essential. I have many times spent time with people and felt that I have been totally inadequate and unable to establish any contact. I have inwardly despaired and longed for the clock to tick on so that I could leave. Such feelings are common and understandable, and we need to 'offer up' the situation. Remember the old adage – your best is always good enough for God, and if you are doing your best, with sensitivity and compassion, then you can do no more. But we do need to be

---

[26] Published in 1998 by Methodist Homes for the Aged in co-operation with The Christian Council on Ageing. Epworth House, Stuart Street, Derby DE1 2EQ

doing our best, our second best is not enough. Try to ensure that you have the time and the space for the visit, give it your full attention, and do not go with feelings of resentment. The visit must be an event in its own right. It is not intended to be a support to your own sense of worth but to bring a fresh voice and face and occasionally, we hope, a sense of the divine to someone who may be trapped in their home and in their sense of isolation.

Christian ministry does not have to use religious language. We must not assume that visits have to have a specifically 'religious' content in order for them to be appropriate or authentic. Sometimes a prayer or a reflection on the scriptures is what is needed and is entirely appropriate, very often it is not. Much will depend upon the background and tradition of the person with dementia, and also upon the understanding upon which the visit is based. When a minister visits, having previously arranged with the carers and the person concerned, to take communion, this will clearly be what is expected and what may well be needed. For someone else or on another occasion the conversation may be about the old days, gardens, fishing, market days or any other subject – they are all part of God's world and they are all capable of becoming vehicles for loving acceptance and enjoyable stimulation.

In the earlier stages of the illness the person may wish to share with you something of their concerns and their fears. Take those concerns seriously and do not try to dismiss or minimalise them. The future may be bleak and it is no use suggesting that everything will be just fine. The honest response is to try and listen to their fears and, with them, to see if there might be any ways in which such fears may be faced up to, and what sort of help and support might the person feel that they need as they look into the future. The subject and pace here is clearly set by the person with dementia and is not imposed upon them by any visitor, but if the matter is raised, then love requires us to respond with integrity and compassion. How those two factors combine can be very challenging and demanding.

If the person you are visiting lives with their spouse or other family member you need to ascertain whether they are wanting to stay with you during the visit or to leave you together, without them. This may give the carer a few minutes respite. If they choose to stay with you, make every effort to engage with the person with dementia and try not to sit and talk to the carer *about* the person. This can marginalise them and treat them as an object to be talked about, rather than a subject to be engaged with. It may be appropriate on some occasions to talk with the person with dementia and their carers separately, because they may well have different needs. This is a matter of fine judgement.

A home visit to someone with dementia can be a demanding and skilled exercise and it is not something to be embarked upon when your mind is elsewhere or your eye is on the clock. More than most people, people with dementia demand and deserve our total commitment and focus. If we are not prepared to give them our all, then it is better not to visit now and to choose a different time.

Visiting nursing homes

I have already mentioned the work of John Killick, who spends many hours with people with dementia and engages with them, writing down the words that they say. He then turns their actual words into poems which, he believes, convey what the people were endeavouring to tell him. One of his most powerful poems concerns a nursing home:

God so loved the world
but He did not love this place.
All I want to do is die.
So why can't I be let to do so?
Why can't you just lay down your head?

I walk and walk and walk
but there is no God,
not in this place.
This is The Bad Home –
He has forgotten its existence.

I get up and walk till I fall.
Sinful though I be
I'll ask God for His mercy.
I'm too old to do anything.
I'm just a dustbin.

It's all the same here.
Some of the girls grasp you
as if you're a cat or a dog.
They're too young. They can't
understand the problems of age.

It's all the same here.
They're so busy,
they'll help you into anything,
even rags. You're not a person
when you come in here.

Nothing to do, nothing to say.
It's all blackness in front of me.
Another thing, they just sit there
and turn their thoughts inward.
That's why we'll never get better.

God so loved the world
but He doesn't love me.
I used to be happy,
but now I'm angry with Him
because I'm still here.   (Killick 2000)

Moving into a nursing home can be a very difficult and emotional decision, both for the people with dementia and for their families. There will inevitably be a whole range of mixed feelings, anger, relief, guilt, fear, a sense of failure and perhaps a feeling of being abandoned or of abandoning. Very often all these feelings are there in the one person. For some people, arranging for their husband or wife, their mother or their father to go into nursing care is just about the worst thing that they have ever had to do. Reflecting on this one American writer (Renee Shield 1997) comments that the nursing home:

> symbolically embodies the dangerous transition from adulthood to death. It is cut off, clearly bounded and separated from 'normal' life on the outside. The nursing home residents, tainted as they are by their nearness to death, cannot spread it to those in the community because of the separation.

And yet, we also know that a nursing home can provide the care and security, the professional attention and twenty-four hour care which is quite beyond the scope of most families to provide. Nevertheless, it can be a time of considerable tension and sadness. A great many tears have been shed over this particular stage in the life of many people with dementia. Both they and their families are in need of tender support, and it is a support which needs to continue.

I have never come across any simple *Service of Admission* into a nursing home, and I have never used one myself, but if I were starting out on ministry again I think I would use such a service where it was appropriate. I have drafted the sort of thing I have in mind and it can be found in Appendix A on page 213. It is a shared and symbolic way of recognising the transition from one stage of life to another, it recognises the mixed emotions that are around and seeks to be open about our hopes and fears for the future. It is the sort of thing which could be left by a person's bedside and they might possibly read it now and again, or visitors could read it, or parts of it, with the person concerned. Clearly it would not be appropriate to use such a service with everyone, but it could provide comfort and a particular context which might be helpful to some people as a formal recognition of a rite of passage.

I did come across a 'Service of Thanksgiving and Remembrance for Family Carers of People with Dementia in Residential Care' when visiting Australia, and I have drafted something along these lines which might be helpful to some people, and this can be found in Appendix B on page 217. It could be used on a quarterly or an annual basis.

There is a specific ministry to people with dementia in nursing homes, people who may be members of our faith community or relatives of our members; this is a visit to a particular person. There is also a more generalised ministry to nursing homes themselves, to the whole community, either as chaplain, local priest or minister or on some other basis. Some larger nursing homes and also homes administered by religious communities often have their own chaplains, and may even have their own chapel or 'sacred space'. Most nursing homes though, certainly in Britain, tend to be smaller, privately run homes, and few of these have any formal links with local churches or have a chaplain. However, as there is more and more emphasis now being placed upon the spiritual care of residents, the time may be ripe for local clergy or churches to make enquiries as to whether there might be some value in formalising an ongoing link.

In our increasingly secular society it may be quite difficult for people to know just what is envisaged by a chaplaincy link, or by some kind of ongoing arrangement with a local church. It is quite possible that the local church doesn't quite know how to approach the nursing home, or what to offer, and the nursing home may have little understanding of what a local church can provide, or how to go about making enquiries. There is often a deep chasm between the two, caused by mutual ignorance and incomprehension of the other. I have come across a few examples of 'contracts' agreed by local churches and nursing homes, and I give an example of these in Appendix C on page 221.

It needs to be clearly understood by both sides that the churches are not viewing the nursing home as a mission field, as a place to gather converts or, in any ways whatsoever, to take advantage or apply 'spiritual' or any other sort of pressure on people who are very vulnerable. The church's motive must always be one of compassionate service, in which people are honoured and no attempt is made to proselytise or cajole. I will discuss the role of worship in the next chapter.

It can be quite a devastating experience to be admitted into a nursing home, even if it is very good one. There are many good ones but, sadly, there are also a great many which leave much to be desired. The economics of an ageing population is an increasingly difficult subject for governments to handle, and the economics of residential care forms a part of this whole scenario. Many homes struggle to remain profitable. They are often based in uneconomic buildings, face problems recruiting and retaining appropriate staff and, because of these and many other pressures, there is all too often a culture in which the resident needs to fit in with the home rather than the home be based around the resident.

Small units often do not have sufficient flexibility of staff and therefore training and staff development becomes a low priority. But it is not only a matter of size, it is ultimately a matter of commitment and attitude, and not all homes have even begun to embrace the new culture of dementia care. Sadly, many people will recognise the scenario set out in John Killick's poem earlier in this chapter. To get some idea of what it can be like to find oneself in such an institution, or how it is in hospital, it is worth reading two novels and then reflecting on how real they seem to you in your experience. I would suggest *As We Are Now* by May Sarton (1983) and *Moon Tiger* by Penelope Lively (1987)

As Marita Grudzen (2003) reminds us:

In the course of ageing, ordinary daily events of life typically acquire greater significance. People's lives become more circumscribed and their energy more limited. They also become vulnerable to pain and to loss of privacy. The person who has little independence and is unable to perform the activities of daily living (e.g. eating, toileting, bathing, grooming, transporting to and from a chair) experiences a profound loss of control ..... the institutional character of a long-term care setting may exacerbate a person's feelings of loss.

It can be very difficult to adjust to communal living after many years of being independent. There is a great temptation for places to adjust to the lowest common denominator and to provide services and diversions which can be quite alienating for many people. People can be terribly lonely in the midst of a community if they do not share the underlying culture. Sharon Waller (2002b) writes of her experience of a nursing home:

> In the last year of my father's life I don't believe that he shared the same culture as the people around him which I can only imagine as a great loneliness. Ethicist Stephen Post (1995) calls this a "terrible breaking off from the values of dominant culture" (p29)

Just as earlier I pointed out that the great challenge is to see not a person with *DEMENTIA*, but a *PERSON* with dementia, so there is a similar challenge to our society to provide nursing *HOMES* rather than *NURSING* homes. A helpful book to encourage us in that process is *Vital Connections in long-term care* by Barton, Grudzen and Zielske (2003). When my father in law died a few years ago, he had been living in a residential home for several years, after the death of his wife who had dementia. When it came to arranging his funeral it was agreed that the family should gather at the place where he lived, and the hearse left from the residential home even though he had died in hospital, and the staff gathered at the door to see him off. It was after all, *his home.*

Visiting hospitals

People with dementia who are in hospital are either there because they have had a fall and/or have some illness, or because they are in a long-stay ward. It is often, regrettably an experience of 'warehousing', of keeping a person because there is nowhere else for them to go, but with them receiving little or no treatment or stimulation and often being heavily sedated.

It can be a time of great sadness for the person with dementia, and many of them become more and more withdrawn. It can also be a time of great sadness for their relatives, who may find it increasingly difficult to make meaningful contact with them and who often feel that they are visiting in a somewhat 'alien' environment. If the visitors feel estranged and institutionalised, one can only imagine what the person with dementia might feel.

The church can sometimes find it quite difficult to get involved in this scene, particularly if they did not know the person very well beforehand. It is often left to just one or two people to follow up a referral and one of these is usually the minister, who may or may not find such visiting easy. Eileen Shamy (2003) recounts her first experience of such visiting rather graphically

> I felt an enormous and paralysing burden of helplessness, personal inadequacy and utter and absolute uselessness. It was a devastating experience and I ... wanted to run away.. . . no wonder so many parish clergy are slow to offer pastoral care of a spiritual nature to people with dementia, the risk to self-confidence can be too great.

The local minister therefore can find such visits extremely difficult to handle. Already busy, he or she has probably made a journey of several miles to the hospital, found it difficult to park and almost as difficult to locate the ward. Once there, he or she is invariably directed to a bedside or a chair, perhaps surrounded by many other people, and left to get on with the visit – probably without being offered a seat. It takes considerable courage, imagination and faith to make such a visit an authentic pastoral encounter.

- Make sure that you introduce yourself clearly and fully; you might need to explain that you have come from St Cuthbert's or from the church in the village; you need to ensure that you have given them your name – and allowed all this to have time to register. This visit may have been on your mind for some time, but the person you are visiting may have had no chance to 'think themselves into it', they may even have been dozing off when you arrived.

- Do you have some understanding of how advanced their illness is? Dementia can progress quite slowly. It is important that we visit people expecting there to be some sort of real encounter, but the ways in which that encounter may be established and experienced may have much to do with the person's level of disability. The temptation to be nihilistic must be resisted at all costs!

- Is it appropriate to see if you can move into a more private place? A dayroom, or drawing the curtains ? This has the effect of filtering out some of the distractions and therefore making it easier for the person with dementia.

- What topics are likely to be of interest? What news or information can you bring about – gardens? Football? Shopping? Family? The local community? Reading? Church news? The fact that someone has dementia does not mean that they have become moronic; it may be possible to re-awaken their interest in poetry or history, science or whatever. I remember visiting an elderly lady who engaged me (far beyond my depth!) in a discussion on the metaphysical poets.

- Are there any opportunities for appropriate touch? Sitting quietly holding an elderly man's hand may be much more meaningful than heroic attempts at conversation; or it may, in fact, assist conversation. Women may like to have face cream applied, their hair brushed, or their feet massaged (and so may men!)

▪ Would it be appropriate to take something with you as you visit? Flowers, food, pictures or photographs. One winter's day my colleague took a lady a box full of snow – she loved it! Can you take something that can be left with them after your visit?

▪ Whilst it is right that you work at communicating, always remember that to sit in silence can also be a form of communication. It can be reassuring, not stressful, and emotionally very satisfying if done positively and not out of desperation!

▪ Remember that you do not go alone. You have a representative role and you are bringing to the person some sort of remembrance of the local community, the local and wider church, and God. On behalf of them all you are telling the person with dementia that they are not forgotten. After your visit you can inform people in the local community and in the church, keeping them up to date with the person's news and health, and the visit can serve to inform and illuminate your own prayers and the prayers of your community.

▪ Your visit can also be the occasion for silent prayer, as you sit alongside the person. Often I have been unable to communicate verbally, but by sitting with a person, holding their hand and just being there and reflecting upon the presence of God in that situation, I believe that the visit has been of value. For some people, it may be appropriate to read some verses of a hymn or of scripture; but a visit can be just as 'spiritual' without that; it is a matter of judgement.

- I always indicate when I am about to leave, and invariably give the blessing, placing my hands upon their head. A time for remembering family and friends, for commending the ward and the people to God, and assuring the person with dementia of the abiding presence and love of God.

- It is not always possible to speak to people concerned with providing care, but it is helpful, if possible, to receive some kind of update on how things are going. Often it is possible to share some insights or give some background information which might add to the quality of care.

- If at all possible try to establish a regular and reliable pattern of visiting. Trial and error will help you to work out whether it is better to go in the morning or afternoon and before or after meals. People are often much more communicative and approachable at certain times of the day. Perhaps the most appropriate time is something that can be negotiated with the staff.

- The journey home gives time for reflection and prayer.

Perhaps all this can be summed up in Barbara Beuler Wegner's 'Beatitudes for the Elderly' [27]

Blessed are they who understand
My faltering steps and shaking hand.
Blessed, they who know my ears today
Must strain to catch the words they say.
Blessed are they with a cheery smile
Who stop to chat for a little while.
Blessed are they who never say
'You've told us that story twice today'.
Blessed are they who make it known
That I'm loved, respected and not alone.

---

[27] I have been unable to find the source for this verse, but discovered it quoted in David Stoter's *Spiritual Aspects of Health Care*

Carers within hospitals and nursing homes

Everything in this chapter so far, apart from John Killick's poem, has been written from the perspective of a Christian minister visiting, from the outside. But what of those who work on the inside? As in so many other cases, the most effective form of Christian ministry is provided by those who are there on the spot, day by day, rather than by those who come in from the outside on an occasional basis, important and useful though that may well be. I cannot over-emphasise the crucial work that the care-giver, be it a family member or a paid worker in a hospital, nursing home or day care centre does. Christian ministry is almost always undertaken most effectively by ordinary lay people going about their daily business. The contribution that people make in caring for people with dementia can be a wonderful testimony to the compassionate presence of God, and there are countless examples of it to be found. Such people need to be supported, encouraged and recognised as genuine and authentic vehicles of God's love. It also needs to be understood and accepted that they may well grow weary, they may lose heart on occasion and bear many pains and sufferings, some of which they will never share with anyone. Also, they may well experience feelings of guilt and anger – anger towards God, towards the church and its ministry and towards the person they are caring for. There is a real task for church communities to give support to those who are on the front line, it can be very lonely and very demanding.

Many congregations will contain people who work in hospitals and nursing homes. They will be at the cutting edge of the confrontation between the old culture of dementia care, which focuses upon the medical aspect and upon what people can no longer do, and the new culture, which is person-centred and focuses upon what people are still able to do. It is not a comfortable place to be, as Faith Gibson (1999) points out, but to fail to take on board the new insights of person-centred care, and to act positively in the light of them, can be very destructive for the people that they are caring for:

The consequences of doing nothing, however, are not neutral. Inaction conveys not nothing, but rather the destructive message that the person with dementia is not worth bothering with and is, in fact, a non-person, an object, an it. . . . I do believe that to do nothing consigns the person with dementia to solitary confinement, albeit lived out in the presence of others this is the biggest risk of all.

There is also a price to be paid by staff who risk person-centred communication. There is our own fear of being overwhelmed by the vast morass of unmet need and anxiety about our own future. Tom Kitwood had to face this in himself and wrote: "there is a great deal of anxiety and distress ... I had to face up to and work through my own fears about ageing and developing dementia".

Dementia care requires us to lower our own defences, to come to terms with our own ageing, possible dementia and certain death. It also requires us to get close to people who may be very troubled and very troubling. Person-centred communication is not costless in terms of physical and emotional wear and tear. Not everyone is suited to the demands it makes, or is able to meet those demands at certain times in their lives when other pressures distract, pre-occupy or leave them with depleted energy.

This is also true of family carers, and some are not able to bear the burden or cope with the stresses. The church must not be judgmental in those circumstances, only God knows the full story and understands all the pains. Our role is to provide support, encouragement and all the comforts of Christian ministry to people who may be deeply pained, worried and fearful about the future. I am not advocating an easy 'anything is alright' attitude here, rather I am suggesting that Christian ministry stands alongside people as they struggle, to find the right way ahead for the people they care for, and for themselves. Perhaps asking pertinent questions, compassionately challenging and helping them to reach a mature judgement about their own situation.

An encouragement for carers in institutions

A few years ago I was asked to spend time in Australia visiting various nursing homes and other complexes looking after people with dementia. Towards the end of my stay I was asked to preach at the annual service at Wesley Gardens in the outskirts of Sydney and I tried to reflect on all the work I had seen in the previous weeks and sum up what I thought it was all about. I chose as the reading the story from the Gospels (Luke 5v17-26) in which a group of friends bring their sick companion to Jesus only to find that there were too many people about and they couldn't reach him. They moved into 'plan B' and went up on the roof and lowered their friend down through the open space to be found in houses at that time. Jesus was impressed by their imagination, determination and by their faith, and their friend received healing. This is what I said:

"I want to begin by sharing with you two images.

The first concerns my visit to an orchestral concert in the Sydney Opera House the other evening. It was a special concert, celebrating the Paralympic Games and there were a hundred or more people in wheelchairs attending and enjoying the music. There was a piano concerto included in the programme and the soloist was the French pianist Bernard D'Ascoli. He had to be escorted to the piano and on and off the platform as he is either blind or has extremely bad eyesight. He played beautifully, and no doubt all those people in wheelchairs will be amazing people over the next couple of weeks as they take part in these international games. The evening brought home to me two things; first that we should never underestimate the potential of people with handicaps. Then secondly, it reminded me once again that all of us are handicapped in one way or another – some more noticeably than others, but there is none of us without some form of handicap.

My second image is that of my mother, (who died twenty two years ago yesterday), desperately ill in hospital. At one of the lowest points in her illness a student nurse sat with her through the night and comforted her. Although it was all those years ago, I have never forgotten that act of kindness. You see, our acts of mercy, love and friendship are not in vain and are not forgotten, even though we ourselves may never know anything more about them.

Now let me go back to the story from Luke's Gospel. I want you to try and imagine yourself into that little episode. Your friend is in need, he has some form of illness and it is beyond your resources to meet his needs. You hear that someone is in town who might just be able to help, but you don't really know, so you decide to risk it and carry your friend to where Jesus is staying. Now that's not an easy task and there are several obstacles to be overcome. They didn't have forms to fill-in in those days but getting through the crowds to reach Jesus wasn't easy. That's why you hit upon the ingenious idea of lowering him through the roof.

These friends were at their wits end, and in the encounter with Jesus, something happened. We don't really know what it was all about and how it happened, but some sort of healing took place. Now note, it had nothing to do with the man's faith or belief systems, we know nothing about them. But his friends believed that this was a worthwhile thing to do. And isn't that what happens here? People are brought into your care because their friends and relatives don't quite know what to do and they believe that in some way bringing them to you will help.

It is not easy work that you are involved in. It can be tiring and costly. It can drain you, tax your reserves. We had a workshop in this room on Friday on staff burn-out and people shared with each other some of their strategies for coping – including taking a double-bath with champagne, which I thought was quite a freed-up strategy. However, I hadn't understood the accent. What they were actually talking about was taking a *bubble* bath with champagne – but who knows, we may have hit upon a new strategy!

Now just as people get burnt out in the ways that they were all discussing, they can also get a form of spiritual burn-out, though they may not describe it as such. One of the great theologians of the post-war world is Jurgen Moltmann, and he wrote a wonderful article that I read about forty years ago and which I have never forgotten, though I have long since forgotten where I read it. He wrote about how we meet up with the glory of Christ in our worship, our sacraments, our fellowship and our scriptures. Here, within the traditions of the church it is possible to catch glimpses of Christ in Majesty – like some of the statues and paintings in our churches. But we are not meant to stay forever in church, we are called out into a broken and suffering world, to meet and to minister to the Christ who comes to us on the edges, in pain, forsaken and bewildered. And as we seek to tend to the bruises and hurts of the Christ who dwells incognito amidst the poor and the lowly, so we get drained, so we get tired and so we lose the conviction that it is Christ whom we are serving. We therefore need to return to those places and those people who reveal to us Christ in Majesty. But once we have caught sight of the glory of Christ, so we are propelled back into the world of pain in order to recognise him afresh in the bodies and the faces and the situations of the people whom we meet day by day. It is what I call ping-pong theology, and it is a vital part of our life.

You are all entrusted with work of great importance. But you too are fragile and vulnerable people. Paul spoke about having this treasure in earthen vessels, and isn't that our experience?

To get to know a facility like Wesley Gardens is to realise what a large number of people are involved in this work. Board members, senior staff, admin people, nursing and care staff, caterers, people in the laundry, educators, ministers, therapists, volunteers, auxiliaries . . . everyone!

And from the perspective of Faith we are also all involved. Christian ministry is not simply reserved for those who are especially pious or for those who have great faith (though I am not wanting to belittle piety or faith!). Remember the people whom

Jesus drew to himself – they were seldom the high-born intellectuals, the priests or the religious leaders. He called working people, fishermen, tax-collectors, shepherds. He called the impetuous Peter, doubters like Thomas, sensuous people like Mary Magdalene, busy people and reflective people like Mary and Martha; single-minded and argumentative types like Paul. And he called a multitude of people who were so 'ordinary' that we know nothing about them.

The point I am making is this. *You* are the people who have been called into and chosen for this special ministry to those who are the least of his brethren. 'Called', 'Chosen' and 'Ministry' are my words. Other people might say that you are the ones who responded to the advertisement or the phone call, you got through the interview; you are working to earn some money to pay the mortgage, feed the kids or pay for that special holiday. It's the same thing, but looked at from a different perspective, from a different angle.

You may be looking after that difficult and argumentative Mr Burns, that incontinent Mrs Jones, the weeping Jim or the almost incomprehensible Juliet – but the eyes of faith see you ministering to the broken body and mind of Jesus. You are nurses and therapists, administrators and cleaners, but you are also ministers of a Gospel of love and acceptance, of care and compassion.

It matters not that you are not always sure about what you believe, or that you are struggling with anxieties or that you get depressed. It matters not that your kids are playing up or that your marriage is under strain. Of course you have problems, of course you are less than perfect, of course you have hopes and fears, good days and bad – you are human! You are part of that great mass of men and women who catch occasional glimpses of glory, recognise moments of grace and for most of the time get on with your working and your living. The writer of the book *Ecclesiasticus* says of such people

> they maintain the fabric of this world
> and their work is their prayer.

It is part of the mystery and glory of God that such people are chosen to be channels of his grace.

> Christ has no body now on earth but yours
> No hands but yours
> No feet but yours
> Yours are the eyes through which he looks
> with compassion on the world
> Yours are the feet with which he is to go about
> doing good
> and yours are the hands with which he is
> able to bless us now (St Teresa of Avila)

Perhaps as an outsider I can say something on behalf of all the people for whom you care. It is sometimes easier for an outsider to see the overall picture, it is rather like tapestry. You are all on the one side and consequently you see all the overlapping threads, the knots, the loose ends and all the confusions- the back of the tapestry is seldom beautiful. But I am on the other side, and I see the whole picture, the patterns, the different colours and textures. I see something of the beauty, and I want to say 'Thank You'.

You are the living proof that 'no man is an island entire unto himself', for by your work you demonstrate that we all belong to each other. Let me close with an adaptation of a famous prayer:

> God be in your head and in your understanding
> God be in your eyes and in your looking
> God be in your mouths and in your speaking
> God be in your hearts and in you thinking
> God be at your end and at your departing –
> and at the departing of all those people who
> have been brought to you,
> for your love,
> for your care and for your skills.
>   Amen

A final word

Two of the questions that I hear so often from people who seek to engage in some form of ministry to and with people with dementia are 'is it worth the effort? and 'does it do any good?' Christine Bryden (2002) is an Australian Anglican who has Alzheimer's and she gave a very moving address at a conference (please note!) which was later published. She said:

> Where does this journey begin and at what stage can you deny me my selfhood and my spirituality? . .. As I lose an identity in the world around me, which is so anxious to define me by what I do and say, rather than who I am, I can seek an identity by simply being me, a person created in the image of God. My spiritual self is reflected in the divine and given meaning as a transcendent being . . . As I travel toward the dissolution of my self, my personality, my very 'essence', my relationship with God needs increasing support from you, my other in the body of Christ. Don't abandon me at any stage, for the Holy Spirit connects us. It links our souls, our spirits – not our minds or brains. I need you to minister to me, to sing with me, pray with me, to be my memory for me. . . . You play a vital role in relating to the soul within me, connecting at this eternal level. Sing alongside me, touch me, pray with me, reassure me of your presence, and through you of Christ's presence.

Earlier, in the same talk Christine said

> I need you to be the Christ-light for me, to affirm my identity and walk alongside me. I may not be able to affirm you, to remember who you are or whether you visited me. But you have brought Christ to me. If I enjoy your visit, why must I remember it? Why must I remember who you are? Is this just to satisfy your OWN need for identity? So please allow Christ to work through you. Let me live in the present. If I forget a pleasant memory, it does not mean that it was not important for me.

God was in Christ, reconciling the world to himself.
May God also be in us, continuing that work of reconciliation.
May we see Christ in people with dementia
     as they seek to reconcile their fragmenting understanding
     with all the confusing activities of the world around them.

Lord, as I move into an uncertain future
     provide me with those who can be the
     Christ-light for me.
Enfold me within the worshipping community and
     help me to rest in the faith that
     although I may well forget you,
     your love never allows you to forget me.
Thank you, for that good news, that Gospel message
     which will sustain my inner being, even though
     I may be unable to remember from whom
     Such love and mercy flows.

Chapter 11

Worship –Problems and Possibilities

How can we sing the songs of the Lord while in a foreign land? The problem faced by the writer of Psalm 137 is faced by just about everyone who is engaged in the process of providing formal worship opportunities for people with dementia. There are, of course, many ways in which people worship God, many ways to reflect on the blessings and mercies of life, many ways to express wonder and gratitude, many ways to formulate the inner longings of our heart and soul. But what about formal worship, the ongoing ministry of the church, worshipping alongside others and receiving the sacraments? There are real problems to be faced, but rarely are they insurmountable. I would not necessarily put it in these words, but I understand what Fisher (1990) is trying to say:

> It takes patience, knowledge of the disease, a tub full of love and acceptance of failure to minister to the demented person. There will be times when nothing a chaplain tries can reach them. Not even the Spirit of God can penetrate their troubled minds. The chaplain must adjust his/her style, change his/her mind, study, develop new techniques, use all available resources, be creative and use all their God-given, as well as acquired, gifts in assisting these struggling souls in maintaining a relationship with God.

I believe however, that there is no-one of whom it can be said that 'the Spirit of God cannot penetrate their troubled minds', and I believe that the onus is not on us - or upon them - to maintain a relationship with God. That relationship already exists, though it may not be acknowledged either consciously or unconsciously. It may not be enjoyed. But that is a very different thing to believing that such a relationship does not exist and that it might be our responsibility to help establish it. Our task is surely to help nourish, reinforce and celebrate that relationship and, by sharing in the corporate worship of the church, demonstrate our conviction that people with dementia continue to belong to the whole people of God. Just how we do this presents us with a whole range of problems – and possibilities.

First, we must believe that it is possible. Without such a basic conviction we shall almost certainly find reasons and examples which would suggest that it is not; but it is. Oliver Sacks (1985) recounts the story of Jimmie, who was "charming, intelligent and memoryless" and had been admitted to the Homes for the Aged with a transfer note saying "Helpless, demented, confused and disoriented". Sacks writes that "none of us had ever encountered, even imagined, such a power of amnesia, the possibility of a pit into which everything, every experience, every event, would fathomlessly drop, a bottomless memory-hole that would engulf the whole world". When Sacks raised questions about the basic humanity of Jimmie it was suggested that he should observe him when he went to chapel:

> I did, and I was moved, profoundly moved and impressed, because I saw here an intensity and steadiness of attention and concentration that I had never seen before in him or conceived him capable of. I watched him kneel and take the Sacrament on his tongue, and could not doubt the fullness and totality of Communion, the perfect alignment of his spirit with the spirit of the Mass. Fully, intensely, quietly, in the quietude of absolute concentration and attention, he entered and partook of the Holy Communion. He was wholly held, absorbed by a feeling. There was no forgetting, no Korsakov's then, nor did it seem possible or imaginable that there should be; for he was no longer at the mercy of a faulty and fallible mechanism – that of meaningless sequences and memory traces – but as absorbed in an act, an act of his whole

being, which carried feeling and meaning in an organic continuity and unity, a continuity and unity so seamless it could not permit any break.[28]

Now of course, that little episode is beautifully written up, but many people involved in this type of ministry are able to sharee similar sorts of stories. Not for all people, not for all of the time, but sufficiently frequent for them to press on in faith, believing that 'something' is happening whether it be clearly recognisable or totally hidden. On the other hand, I have heard of clergy who have refused to give Holy Communion to people with dementia because, they claim, the person doesn't understand what is happening. But if 'understanding what is happening' is a pre-requisite for receiving communion would any of us be able to receive?

I am reminded of the occasion when I gave Holy Communion to a lady who was extremely ill. She had been in a dementia unit in a nursing home for many months before I had any knowledge of her existence, but by a circuitous route it came to my knowledge that many years before she had sung in the choir of the church I was then rector of. I have to admit finding my visits to her extremely difficult, and for much of the time I would stand by her bed (with its cot sides raised), hold her hand and silently pray for her as she lay moaning and shouting out. I was never sure if she knew whether I was there or not until one day, after standing like this for about fifteen minutes I said the Lord's Prayer out loud and she said 'Amen'. In subsequent visits I was able to establish some form of spoken communication and, as she approached death I decided to bring her the reserved sacrament. We prayed together and I placed the wafer on her outstretched tongue. A few more prayers and she seemed to drift away into unconsciousness and I prepared to leave. She gave a great sigh, her tongue came out of her mouth and hung down towards her chin and to my consternation I saw that the wafer was still sticking to it. I would like to say, as I recount this story, that with great devotion I

---

[28] I am grateful to Sharon Waller for drawing my attention to this.

removed the wafer and consumed it myself. But I could not bring myself to do that simple task as her mouth was part dry and part frothy. With as much reverence as I could muster I removed the wafer from her tongue, placed it between clean paper tissues and placed it in the waste bin. I recall the incident with a mixture of guilt and embarrassment. The people responsible for my early training in the ministry forty plus years ago would have been horrified, but we learn by our mistakes. I should have communicated her by placing a drop of wine on her lips, but I wasn't imaginative enough to do that. She died a few days later, but I have no doubt that she was received with grace and mercy, as I too hope to be!

In local churches

I have already mentioned, in an earlier chapter, that people are sometimes uneasy or embarrassed when people with dementia appear to act inappropriately in our normal acts of worship. Carers may stop bringing people to church because they neither want to be embarrassed themselves nor do they want the person they have escorted to be a disruption to other people. In this way, very often people slip away from our worshipping communities, sometimes without people really noticing. It is, perhaps, a sad comment on many of our churches that they are unable to accommodate people whose behaviour strays from the norm. I wonder how many people we dissuade from joining us or staying with us as a result of our (often unconscious) desire to have everything 'right' and 'in order'?

One way in which this problem might be addressed if it really does seem that, for whatever reason, it is no longer thought desirable for the person to attend the church's principal services, is to suggest that their carer brings them to church at some other time. They could choose a time when there is no-one else there and the person with dementia would be free to walk around, explore, sing, cry or whatever they wished, without fear of any embarrassment. It might be appropriate for the minister to be there to give a short reading, or it might be possible to sing a hymn or two. In this way, the person's relationship with the physical space remains and it may serve to remind them of so much, and be part of their ongoing spiritual nurturing. It might also provide the nucleus for a small group with similar concerns to meet together.

At home

It will be necessary to work out, in consultation with the person with dementia and their carers how best to serve their worship needs when confined to the house. This is an area that is often ignored either because the minister is not confident enough to know what to suggest or because the people 'do not want to be a nuisance'. They may feel that they are only 'very ordinary' members of the congregation, perhaps not particularly regular in attendance, and so they imagine that some form of service at home is really best suited to those who are especially 'religious'. They may also be quite embarrassed by something which might seem to focus too clearly upon their faith, when they may feel that they have too many doubts to want to engage in a private service. It is important that we do not place burdens upon people, and we need to proceed with caution.

There is a difference between an ordinary pastoral visit and a service and we need to make sure that we don't confuse the two. It may be that the idea of holding a service is only something that is suggested once there has been a regular pattern of pastoral visiting established. It might begin by marking the major festivals, or some significant event in their life such as giving thanks for a Golden Wedding, or for the birth of a great-grandchild. It may also be possible to invite other people along, so that it really does become a corporate event, something which they can share with others. Much will depend upon the circumstances and the sensitivity of the pastoral visitor, be they clergy or lay.

The important thing is that we work hard at ensuring that a person with dementia is not 'excommunicated' because of their disability, and that the compassionate outreach and friendship of the worshipping community continues.

In nursing homes and hospitals

It is often quite difficult to establish a pattern of worship in nursing homes or in hospitals, especially if there is no recognised chaplain. Alison Froggatt (1994) was aware of this when she wrote about meeting people's spiritual needs, in an article in The Journal of Dementia Care:

> Those who have had meaningful religious experiences much earlier in their life benefit from being reminded of their beliefs. This helps to sustain a sense of hopefulness, safety and peace. Staff do much to entertain and stimulate people with failing mental powers. A little more encouragement may be needed to help see the value of worship, particularly if this is personally unfamiliar to the staff.

People from the churches can easily feel that somehow they are intruding into the life and care patterns of a nursing home or hospital ward. Of course, sometimes they may be – it all depends upon how the approach is made. There is a sort of uneasy truce between the different establishments, neither really understanding the other, not wanting to cause offence, but both being unsure how to relate to the other. We need to work towards a pattern being established whereby the hospital or nursing home can appreciate the value of the church's ministry, and see how a regular service, at the very least can provide some stimulation and diversion for people, and often a great deal more than that. Kerrie Hide (2002) suggests that:

> Symbol and ritual can enable those who are most vulnerable, those who no longer have access to analytical language, those who have forgotten the things that their eyes have seen, to be

in touch with and to express what is most sacred and important in their lives.

Clergy and others from the churches can feel themselves marginalised in the total care concept of people in hospitals and nursing homes. They are unsure about how the system operates, who makes decisions and what level of co-operation they can reasonably expect to be afforded to them and how they can express their own needs without appearing to intrude or interfere with the general routine of the ward or home. Staff in the homes or hospitals are also unsure about how to handle some approaches by clergy and local churches. Where there is a resident chaplain the situation is eased somewhat, but certainly for nursing homes, most do not have such an appointment. Grey (1994) discusses this problem and says that there is:

> Little practical guidance available for nurses who wish to understand a patient's spiritual needs and resources. However, if a holistic approach is to be practised, ignoring the spiritual aspects of patients' lives is an omission of care.

The situation has improved somewhat in the years since Grey wrote that; with spiritual care being specifically required by nursing homes now, but there is very mixed evidence about how effective this is, how seriously it is pursued and what training and support is available for staff. Grey was interested in examining just why staff found this area so difficult and amongst his conclusions were the following points

- there is a poor awareness of what spirituality is all about

- staff do not want to appear incompetent and so the area is avoided as much as possible

- they are uncertain about their own personal religious and spiritual beliefs and values

- they may be ill at ease with the situations that sometime bring spiritual matters to the fore

- they may not agree that spirituality is within the domain of nursing care

- they may be stressed, experience a lack of time and therefore give these matters a low priority

- they may feel that they lack the appropriate communicative skills

- they may be much more at home focusing on physical needs

Having said all this, I have invariably found that staff in both hospitals and nursing homes have been extremely courteous, even if they were not at all sure what I might be wanting. On reflection, I have to confess that most of the problems that I encountered were more a result of my own sense of uncertainty as to what was needed and how to go about getting it than any opposition or negativity on the part of the nursing staff. I think this just goes to highlight how difficult an area this is for churches to get established, how much thought and preparation needs to go into the planning and how clear we need to be about our objectives – all points which will be discussed in this next section.

A checklist for services

Before the service

- *What are you hoping to provide?*

The old adage "if you don't know where you're going you are unlikely to arrive" certainly applies here. It is vitally important that we have a clear idea of what we are hoping the service will be and what we hope to achieve in it. Some objectives, I would suggest, are inappropriate for people with dementia, and amongst these I would include the evangelical 'pressing for conversion' approach. We are dealing with extremely vulnerable people and their need for acceptance and reassurance is paramount. We need to have a simple objective, such as 'to celebrate the presence of God', 'to rejoice in God's continuing care' or 'to know that we are loved by God'. In fact these are all immensely profound insights, but they are simple in the sense of being able to be summarised in just a few words. When all is stripped down, when all the accretions of the centuries have been set aside, what is the good news that we wish to share? Surely, that God loves each and every one of us with an abiding and an unconditional love.

- *Prepare it well*

Is the service only for people with dementia or for others as well? The likelihood is that in a hospital ward, it will be just for people with dementia, whilst in most nursing homes there may be a mix of people with dementia and people without. We need to be clear in our mind about the problems and possibilities of mixed or separate services, and make our plans accordingly. There may also be relatives attending.

Do the hymns and readings we have chosen focus upon the objective that we have in mind? Will the words that we speak bring reassurance? Have we sorted out the music, the prayers, the readings and readers? Does everyone who is taking part in leading the service know exactly what they are required to do? Sorting things out in a huddle a few minutes before the service begins is not what I call being prepared. These services need to be as well thought out and prepared as the most well-attended and 'important' services in our church's calendar. People in the community can go elsewhere if they are not fed and nurtured by my church, but they can go nowhere else when they are confined to a hospital ward or a nursing home lounge. A huge responsibility is placed upon our shoulders. I know how easy it is, after a busy day to 'cobble together' a few thoughts for "just a few elderly people"; but second best is never good enough. These people deserve the very best that we can offer.

- *Offer it up, as a precious gift*

The service that we are preparing for these, 'the least of my brethren' needs to be seen as the offering that we bring to the Lord, nothing less. It is the offering of the loaves and fish that we bring to be blessed, in the hope that those around us may be fed. And how great is the hunger and thirst for love and peace and acceptance that we see around us, and how inadequate we are to satisfy such hunger and thirst. We offer it up for their sake, and for ours.

The service itself

- *How will the room be set out?*

It is likely that the service will take place in a ward, lounge or day room. How can this space be transformed into 'church' for this short space of time, because for many of the people this may be the nearest that they are likely to be to a church for the rest of their life. Thought and care needs to be given to how the room can become 'different' from its normal everyday use. For this period of time we wish it to become a 'sacred space', in the hope that somehow, it might help people to discover and experience other sacred spaces in their daily lives.

If chairs are to be set out, you will need to arrive early, and it needs to be clearly understood whose responsibility it is to prepare the room. This is something that will need to be discussed and agreed with the staff. It is very difficult to arrive at the room and to find it being used for something else, or to have to move people out or interrupt something that may be going on before you arrive. A helpful and supportive staff will ensure that the room is available for you and will not leave you alone to move people out. If you are able to establish a regular pattern then this is something that can be put in their diary in advance. It might, as a precaution, be worthwhile phoning them up an hour or so beforehand to remind them that you are coming. With people working shifts it is quite likely that the person you discussed it with the last time you were there is not on duty the next time you go. It is an area where there can be friction because of a lack of understanding or communication, so be warned!

- *What type of service is it to be?*

Whatever type of service we eventually settle upon, there is value in ensuring that there is a sense of continuity and repetition from one service to another. Commenting on this, Margaret Goodall (1999), a Methodist minister wrote:

> In the Free Church tradition, leaders of worship are encouraged to use variety in their choice of hymns and prayers, in order to engage the imagination of the congregation and give life to the worship. At Westbury (A Methodist Home for the Aged for those with dementia) the opposite seems to be true. We came to realise that what appears to be needed is consistency and repetition, which then becomes a familiar framework for this special time together.

Margaret outlines the format of a service that has proved beneficial in her work, as does Eileen Shamy (2003). Whilst it is helpful to reflect on the work of others, it is probably easier to devise your own service, so that you can 'live with it' and have the confidence that it expresses the message and tone that you are trying to communicate. If your tradition is to focus upon Eucharistic worship, then the service will probably need to be shortened considerably. The prayers should resonate with those in use sixty to seventy years ago and not be the modern versions, because people with dementia may have forgotten them. Some people find it helpful to have the service printed out in a way that is easy to read and understand, other people prefer not to have a printed form. If you wish to follow a printed service you might get the sheets laminated so that they are always fresh and clean to use. I have seen such sheets using different colours to make it easier for people to know which parts they speak and which parts are to be spoken by the leader. If you are inclined to follow that path, take advice from professionals working in the field regarding what size and colours are easiest for people with dementia or elderly people to read.

- *Are the music and words of the hymns familiar?*

In the last twenty or thirty years there has been a great resurgence in hymn-writing and we now have some truly excellent contemporary hymns. It is unlikely, however, that they will be of much help in services for people with dementia. It is advisable to draw up a list of the 'old favourites' and to concentrate on them. If you are using a hymn book, try to make sure that it is user friendly, there are now one or two hymn books especially designed for use in hospitals, these may or may not suit your purposes. It is probable that you may find the most helpful way forward is to print out the two or three hymns you propose to use for each service on a separate sheet – using large type! This gets over the problem of trying to find No.123 and then No.68, and so on. In general terms, hymns with fifteen verses should be avoided.

Similar comments can be made about the music. Old traditional tunes, the ones they may have known in their childhood and youth are much to be preferred rather than modern versions which may be very acceptable in a family service in the local church but will invariably be greeted with blank looks from members of this particular congregation. Music is important in this context. It has been observed that as dementia progresses and people continue to lose their skills and faculties, a sense of rhythm is just about the last thing to disappear. Also, it is not uncommon to find that people who can no longer engage in any form of extended conversation are still able to sing or recite hymns and prayers with little apparent difficulty. If our services enable people to become involved and engaged then they will be doing something very wholesome and restorative for them.

If it is possible to bring an organist, pianist or keyboard player with you to each service, that will be a great bonus. Live music enhances the sense of worship and also provides a sense of team effort on the part of those leading the worship. Many nursing homes have a piano in their lounge, although you are unlikely to find one in most hospital wards. If there is no access to live music then there are a number of hymns on cassette[29] which are now available commercially. If these are to be used it is essential that the right place is found on the cassette so that you are not left fumbling around in the middle of the service. Also check that the number of verses on the cassette corresponds to the number of verses on your hymn sheet!

It may be unrealistic to bring a church choir to these services on a regular basis, but if they could accompany you at Christmas and Easter then it serves to reinforce the 'special nature' of those Festivals. Many people find that there are one or two people in their congregation who are willing to accompany them to such services on a regular basis and this can be of enormous value and support. Not only do they 'keep the singing going' and help maintain the structure of the service, but they can also sit alongside people and support and encourage them. Building up a small team of people who will share in this ministry reduces the loneliness that an isolated minister can feel, but also underlines the fact that this is a shared ministry within the church and makes good theological sense. On the other hand, it is important that people are not confused about who is leading the worship and there is much to be said for familiarity and continuity. Revolving leadership may be the right thing to do in many situations, but in dementia care it is probably more appropriate that just one person can readily be identified as the person who is fulfilling this leadership role. This will usually, though not always, be the ordained minister.

- *Reading from the Scriptures*

There are three main points that we need to bear in mind

---

[29] Such as *Loving Kindness* which can be ordered from the Dementia Services Development Centre at the University of Stirling.

❑ Use familiar passages – well known stories or verses

❑ Read from versions which the people are likely to know

❑ Keep the reading short – better to have two short readings than one long one. People with dementia do not usually have long concentration spans; nor do they handle complex sentences very well.

Can any of the members of the congregation share in the reading? If so, do you have a large-print version of the Bible handy in case they may need it?

▪ *What symbols will you be using?*

There are many ways in which communication takes place and the spoken word is but one of them. The Christian church has a long history of providing visual and auditory cues, to help us focus our hearts and minds on the mystery of God. We need to think through how we might import some of this symbolic communication into our worship.

Many people find it helps if they set out an altar or a communion table, with perhaps a cross and candles on it. Space, or the tradition you come from, may persuade you that this is not appropriate. Sometimes an open Bible may be placed on the table, or communion vessels if the service is to be Holy Communion. Whatever you decide, the important thing is that you have given some thought as to what the focus of the group is likely to be, and you have good reasons for deciding things in the way that you have. Some people may bring in banners, although I have not had experience of that myself. But are there any visual signs for people to pick up, so that they realise that this is not just the day room or the ward, but is now a formal place of worship. I realise that worship can take place in these rooms day in and day out, but is there anything that now suggests that this is somehow a different time, a time of corporate and shared exploration and celebration of faith? Margaret Goodall (1999) says:

We believed that it was important to make use of signs and symbols that would either cue in memories of other services the residents had attended or feed some aspect of their spiritual lives. They are important as ways into the imagination and memory; in fact. 'Not to use symbols ... in liturgy ... is to fight with one hand tied behind one's back'. (Thiselton 1986 p.23)

Different people will reach different decisions regarding what is worn by the person leading the worship. There are good arguments for 'dressing up' and there are good reasons why things should be kept simple. The important thing is that you reach a decision based upon what you believe the service is about, what you are trying to communicate, and what you feel is appropriate. Eileen Shamy (2003) was quite clear about how she saw things:

I always wear my clerical collar, ecumenical alb, stole and cross and observe the colours of the liturgical year when leading worship for people with Alzheimer's Disease ...... it needs to be understood that such memory cues are necessary to help many worshippers cue into 'church'. The nursing home lounge is now the only church space that the residents are likely to experience. I want to do everything possible to make it a holy place of Presence for them. That means clerical dress and vestments, flowers or candles, and a cross on the covered mobile feeding tray likely to be doing duty as an altar or communion table.

I have always tended to the view that it is good to wear a clerical collar even when visiting, because in that way one is immediately recognised by both the staff and the residents. Colleagues have reached a different decision, which just goes to show that there is no one, 'right' way. The ruling principle seems to be that we should do whatever we believe to be in the best interest of the people we are seeking to worship with.

- *No sermon!*

We need to remember that when a person has dementia, the logical, reasoning side of their brain tends to be affected first, and they will find it extremely difficult to follow any lengthy or closely argued address. The emphasis must be upon brevity and simplicity. This is not the same as saying that it needs to be childish, it does not. But we need to discover how to express some of the profound truths of the faith in words and images that are immediate and simple. I think we have an example of that in the New Testament!

Our objective in speaking (briefly) will be to reassure people of God's presence and love, God's mercy and grace. This is neither the time nor the place for speaking about sinfulness or judgement: people need to be reassured about God's presence and love. The time for wrestling with one's conscience has now passed and the time for relaxing and accepting the unconditional love of God is now with us in all its wonderful, mysterious graciousness. Nothing more is needed.

I am not persuaded by David Keck's assertion (Keck 1996) that "Alzheimer's Disease confronts us starkly with the reality of human sin ...... by original sin I mean that none of us had a choice in being born into a deicidal humanity so wretched as to require the cross for its salvation." In my experience Alzheimer's Disease confronts us starkly with the reality of human love and the unconditional love and acceptance of God.

- *Are there any opportunities for physical contact?*

Is it appropriate to share the peace? Is it possible to go round everyone at the end and give them a personal blessing? Is there any way in which objects can be handed round, or any other way in which touch can be incorporated into the service. There may not be, and that is fine, but it is always worth exploring that possibility.

- *Keep it short*

People with dementia may have a poor concentration span and in general terms I would expect a service of thirty minutes to be an absolute maximum and would be aiming at fifteen to twenty minutes. Most people will have had to make some kind of effort to get there and returning to their room or their bed may also be quite an effort. Taking those journeys into consideration you will see how the time quickly builds up.

- *Expect the unexpected!*

This is perhaps the most useful piece of advice I have to offer. In these sort of services anything, really *anything,* can happen and we must hope that we are not too disconcerted or distracted by it all.

I am reminded of an old Chassidic story about a young boy who attended synagogue with his father. Bored and feeling left out, he began to play his flute and the more he played the less aware of the service he became. Eventually he finished playing with a very loud phrase. His father was overwhelmed by embarrassment, seeing all the congregation looking his way, and he began to apologise profusely. The Rabbi stopped him in his tracks and thanked him for the gift of his son. 'I know that we were all praying, but somehow our prayers lacked immediacy. Only now, carried along by your son's music are our prayers accepted by God'.

When people disturb our worship do we believe that they are disturbing God? If not, then surely we can live with it.

After the service

- *Time of reflection*

By yourself, or with any people who were sharing in the leadership of the service with you, spend time reflecting on what seemed to go well and what seemed to be a problem. This time of reflection is as important as the time of preparation, and if you are able to make it a regular occurrence it will assist you in your preparation for the following service. I know that when time is short and other pressures are mounting, it is all so easy to just be thankful that that particular piece of work is over – but it isn't – not until this process of reflection has taken place.

▪ *How do you cope with your feelings of inadequacy?*

Few people feel that they have been very 'successful' in leading worship with people with dementia and in meeting their spiritual needs. We therefore need ways of coming to terms with our sense of inadequacy. We all have different ways of doing this and I am only mentioning it here to assure people that they are not alone when they find this work demanding and feel that they are not very good at it.

▪ *You are working in a difficult area – be thankful for the trust that is placed in you.*

Working with people with dementia really brings home to us the nature of our calling. We have offered ourselves and have tried to mean it when we have said that we would like to go anywhere and do anything in the service of the Lord. Perhaps the sincerity of that act of commitment is now being tested. This is hard work and there are few visible and tangible rewards. Except, that is, the sense of wonder and honour that we are being entrusted with the task of communicating God's love to these, the 'least of my brethren'. There really is a sense of this treasure being contained in earthen vessels, and it is part of our privilege and calling to be sharing in this work.

Funerals

The content of any funeral address for a person with dementia will almost certainly be different depending upon the age of the person who has died. There are a whole range of issues that are normally considered when preparing a funeral for a younger person, irrespective of whether they had dementia or not. If they did have dementia then issues relating to that need to be interwoven with the way in which the death of the younger person is dealt with.

There is often a considerable sense of relief when an elderly person with dementia eventually dies. Relief for the person, who has been unable to lead a normal life, alongside the members of their family and community probably for quite a number of years. Also a sense of relief for the carers who have watched the consequences of this illness with varying degrees of incomprehension and a sense of inadequacy and anxiety, again for quite a long time.

Sometimes the view is expressed that the actual person died a long time ago and all that has died now is the shell which has remained. I believe that such a line of thought should be resisted. The person has *not* died a year or more earlier, they have been stricken by a pernicious illness and they have almost certainly lost all (which is unlikely) or almost all, of their ability to communicate, but they had not died, and I believe that we dishonour the person to suggest that they had. They have had to suffer enough without prematurely being regarded as deceased.

So is there any other way of thinking about them, any other image that we can use which can acknowledge the reality of the distress and sense of loss both of the person with dementia and also of their carers? Whilst it is not easy to come up with anything which seems appropriate (which is why the view of 'dying earlier' is so often used), I think that it is worth exploring the idea of journeying.

The person with dementia has, over a period of time, moved into an area of experience which is to a very large degree, beyond our understanding. They have 'moved on' into a state of living that we can only observe and imagine, but not experience. Recognising that it is vastly different, I think I can also see some connection with Kahlil Gibran's words (1926) on children when he writes:

You may house their bodies but not their souls,
For their souls dwell in the house of tomorrow,
which you cannot visit, not even in your dreams.

I am not suggesting that the experience of dementia is the 'house of tomorrow' (though for some of us it will be just that), but rather that there is a sense of mysterious 'not knowing' what it must be like to be there. That is a very different concept to assuming that the person is dead.

There is much Biblical material on journeying. Some journeys are voluntary and are taken in faith; some are involuntary and may or may not be accompanied by faith. Nonetheless, the idea of moving from where we are into a different place is very much part of the religious tradition that we inherit. What we need assurance about, is whether, in such journeying, we move beyond the scope of God's presence and love. Psalm 139, and many other passages, think otherwise. Paul's great acclamation in Romans is surely apposite to the death of a person with dementia:

Who shall separate us from the love of Christ? Shall tribulation, or distress, or persecution, or famine, or nakedness, or peril or sword? As it is written, 'For thy sake we are killed all the day long; we are accounted as sheep for the slaughter'. Nay, in all these things we are more than conquerors through him that loved us. For I am persuaded, that neither death nor life, nor angels, nor principalities, nor powers, nor things present, nor things to come, nor height, nor depth, nor any other creature, shall be able to separate us from the love of God, which is in Christ Jesus our Lord.

There can be a great vacuum in the lives of carers after such a death, if they have been in the habit of visiting on a regular basis. They may well have fallen out of the habit of attending social events and having days out and holidays. Here again, there is a great opportunity for faith communities to offer friendship and stimulation, activity and, above all, hope.

Suicide

With an increasing number of people receiving an early diagnosis, there is a likelihood that, as the illness progresses, some of them may commit suicide. Our pastoral response in such situation must be especially sensitive and compassionate. For some people, this will have been what they consider to be a final act of love towards their families, wanting to spare them from what they see as the burdens of care. It may also have been an act of considerable courage displaying a determination to exercise some form of autonomy over their lives while they still had the mental capacity to do so.

I am no longer my own but yours.
Put me to what you will,
rank me with whom you will;
put me to doing, put me to suffering;
let me be employed for you or laid aside for you,
exalted for you or brought low for you;
let me be full, let me be empty,
let me have all things, let me have nothing;
I freely and wholeheartedly yield all things to your
   pleasure and disposal.
And now, glorious and blessed God,
Father, Son and Holy Spirit,
you are mine and I am yours.
So be it.
And the covenant made on earth,
let it be ratified in heaven. Amen.[30]

---

[30] Covenant prayer of the Methodist Church

PART FOUR

Theological Reflection

Abide with me; fast falls the eventide
The darkness deepens: Lord with me abide.
When other helpers fail and comforts flee,
Help of the helpless, O abide with me.

Swift to its close ebbs out life's little day;
Earth's joys grow dim; its glories pass away;
Change and decay in all around I see;
O Thou who changest not, abide with me.

Hold Thou thy cross before my closing eyes
Shine through the gloom and
    point me to the skies.
Heaven's morning breaks,
    and earth's vain shadows flee;
In life, in death, O Lord, abide with me.

Henry F Lyte, 1847

Chapter 12
Engage the Mind, Touch the Heart, Feed the Soul

This advertising slogan from the 2003 Edinburgh International Festival – *Engage the mind, touch the heart, feed the soul* - just about encapsulates what I have been trying to do in this book. Any study of dementia is bound to be intellectually demanding. This does not mean that it has to be incomprehensible, but it does entail a considerable amount of reading, reflecting, discussing and arguing. The mind is engaged. It is not an easy subject and we must ensure that we do not trivialise it. But dementia is about people. More than that, it is about people who are hurting, be they the people with dementia or their carers, and it is almost inhuman to confront a person in pain without our heart being touched. For people within communities of faith, and for others, the experience of dementia also raises a host of questions of a spiritual nature – however that word is defined. As we grapple with those questions we often discover that our resources and reserves are low, and somehow we need our souls to be fed. I cannot claim to have achieved all these objectives, but that has been my desire. Throughout this book there has been the underlying question – *How do we sing the Lord's song in a strange land?*

Kevin McKee (1999) wrote words that have remained in my mind for a long time and which encouraged me to set out on this book:

If, as I suspect, there is a connection, and not a discontinuity, between the worlds of those with dementia and those without, and if there is the slightest possibility that a kernel of tranquillity persists at the heart of the chaos of dementia, then we have been culpable in the past of a hideous sin; that of denying humanity to those who, in their vulnerability, are perhaps most human. In so doing we have probably not only exacerbated that vulnerability, but also heightened the terror of the experience.

We are entering into the community of the dispossessed and we need to discover the resources to enable us to approach it with hope and love. It will take time and require graciousness. We shall need to work with gentleness and faith. This is something understood by Debbie Everett (2000) a Canadian hospital chaplain who wrote:

> People with dementia are magic mirrors where I have seen my human condition and have repudiated the commonly held societal values of power and prestige that are unreal and shallow . . . . Because people with dementia have their egos stripped from them, their unconscious comes very close to the surface. They in turn, show us the masks behind which we hide our authentic personhood from the world.

To acknowledge those masks and to face up to our own vulnerability and uncertainty requires a considerable amount of honesty and courage. To take on board the pain and confusion of another person requires similar qualities. To realise that we can learn from them and to recognise that we can still discern their humanity within their disoriented and failing body also requires humility and considerable maturity. But it is also a gift, and we should not condemn those who find such a process impossible.

Construction . . .

To be engaged with people with dementia is to recognise the fragility of the world that most of us have constructed around ourselves. Such constructs, of course, are necessary if we are to survive in our modern complex society and go about doing our daily business, but they are constructs, not reality. Reality is that we are finite and vulnerable. We are bruised and bruising. We are human, which is wonderful, but our lives are of limited duration and we often struggle to survive with dignity and improve and enlighten the lot of others. For people brought up within or choosing to embrace the Christian tradition none of this comes as a great surprise. Our Scriptures are full of passages which seek to remind us both of the glory and yet also of the dependency of our lives. We are lost in wonder and admiration that we should be loved and held by that great mystery whose nature was opened up to us by the life and ministry of Jesus – 'What is man that thou are mindful of him?' asks the Psalmist. It is a question that we ask many times over when confronted by the reality of dementia – what is man, or woman, that they should come to this? How can we affirm and embrace a faith based upon love when we see what can happen to the human mind and to the process of living?

I have outlined elsewhere (Goldsmith1999b) how my involvement with dementia caused me to reconsider many of my theological convictions until I could live with what I considered to be the 'good news' for people with dementia. This challenges the 'gospel' which I believe many of our churches habitually and unreflectingly preach Sunday by Sunday, the gospel which had been at the heart of my life for so many years.

> I am sensing that in coming to grips with the illnesses which cause dementia and in endeavouring to stand alongside those who have them, and in recognising the journey that they (and their carers) are having to make, we are once again being challenged to find a word of hope for the powerless. Theology is being hammered out on the anvil of experience, and the churches are being asked if they have any 'Good News' any Gospel for these, 'the least of my brethren'.

In a world in which 'success' is measured by numbers, by growth, by finance and by power – and it is a world which is not unknown to our churches, for most of them share in it to some degree or other – the experience of dementia represents just about everything that could be described as 'unsuccessful'. We therefore need a theology of patience, of suffering and of 'failure'. We need an open-ended, non-judgmental and merciful theology. Not a theology of certainty, but of tentative exploration, for we are confronted by a strange and foreign world, and it really does challenge us as to whether it is possible to sing the Lord's song in it.

... and deconstruction

The experience of dementia can often herald a process of deconstruction. The deconstruction of many of the myths that surround us and of those which we have willingly promoted or colluded with. Myths about the meaning and purpose of life, which, when we begin to examine them again often leave us feeling bereft and shallow. In addition, for many people there is also a deconstruction of their understanding of God, and of their assumptions about the life of faith and the institution of the church. It can be a time of considerable disillusion, possibly accompanied by anger or depression, or both. It can be a personal experience of the 'dark night of the soul'.

Nothing that I write can take away the pain and sadness associated with dementia. Good dementia care can alleviate some of the suffering and share some of the burden. Skilled support can help us to focus on some of the good things that have happened and indeed, can still continue to happen. It is not all gloom and doom. But there is no escaping the hard reality that this is a progressive illness that will gradually make normal communication more and more difficult. Behaviour may become unpredictable. Memory will slowly evaporate, for some people almost to the point of extinction, and the person will become more and more dependent upon others to meet their almost every need.

It is easy to understand why many people feel that the person has died before their breathing has stopped. But the conviction behind this book is that the person has not died and, awful though this illness is, it is not the dissolution of the person, nor is it necessarily the last word in communicating, living and loving. A further conviction behind this book is that the experience of dementia can lead us into new understandings – about ourselves, about those who are ill, and about the mystery that we call 'God'.

Falling back on our Tradition

There is so much within our Christian tradition to support and encourage us and to illuminate the way as we make that lonely and painful journey through the valley of the shadow of death. The 'dark night of the soul' is part of that tradition. So also are those experiences of helplessness and vulnerability, of hopelessness and despair. We walk along a well-trodden path, one that has been established before us by the saints and martyrs of history. This does not make our journey any easier, but it can be an encouragement to know that we are not alone.

It is interesting to read the Gospels afresh from the perspective of suffering, particularly the Passion narratives[31]. Mark is concerned with the raw, brutal reality. Matthew is concerned about who should carry the blame. Luke is on the look-out for experiences of healing and John gives us a totally new and wider perspective on things. These are all experiences that many of us recognise as we seek to come to terms with the reality of dementia and the particular 'passion' of those whom we care for.

It is the Passion narratives, perhaps more than anything else, which time and time again force us to consider and then reconsider our understanding of suffering. Particularly of 'unmerited suffering' (though that phrase begs the question as to what 'merited suffering' might be). The suffering of Jesus lies at the heart of Christianity, and it is no surprise that the church has never been able satisfactorily to settle on any one definitive understanding of what that suffering was ultimately about. The more we contemplate it, the more we are led further into the mystery of God and the nature of love. Any theological

---

[31] I am indebted to Timothy Tyndall for this insight

exploration of dementia requires us to spend time reflecting upon the Passion narratives.

In our Christian story, the 'agony in the garden', when the disciples were asked to watch and pray as Jesus struggled to discern the way ahead, was followed by betrayal and crucifixion. These are all experiences that have their own particular parallels in the stories of many people with dementia. For Jesus, there then followed a time of waiting, of passivity, as he was taken down from the cross and placed in the grave. It was a time of numbed sensitivity for many of the disciples as they dispersed from Jerusalem and began to make their way home. These experiences too are shared by many of the people with dementia and their carers that we have been thinking about in this book.

At the heart of Christian faith is resurrection. But the mystery and experience of resurrection comes to different people at different times and in different ways, just as it did in New Testament times. The Gospel writers tried to make sense of it in different ways. And so it is for us. For some people a blinding light of understanding and a sense of all things being complete and all things being well. For others, a sense of being supported and accompanied along the way (like the story about the incident on the road to Emmaus), an awareness that life continues and that there can still be hope and meaning and purpose. Some people still wait, unsure, still living in the 'space' between crucifixion and resurrection. The horror and immediate pain of death now in the past but no sense of meaning or hope for living emerging as they resume their daily activities and make their various ways 'home'. And so it is with all grieving, and so it is for those who grieve over the experience of dementia. They may speak a different language, they may use different images, but their experience transcends the cultural and religious boundaries that we have learned to live with day by day. However they may wish to describe it, there is the underlying problem of how do they sing the Lord's song in a strange land?

Can there be hope?

So, is there any word of hope for people with dementia? The answer must be 'Yes, there are many signs of hope'.

There is the hope that as we understand more and more about the condition, so ways of slowing down its progress will become more common and more easily available. The hope that new drugs will emerge which will allow people to live more normal lives for much longer. And the hope that the 'post-code lottery' regarding the availability of drugs that still unfortunately exists in some areas, will be exposed as the cruel and unacceptable practice that it undoubtedly is.

As patterns of care become more developed and the new culture of dementia becomes established in places where the old culture has reigned for so long, so there is hope that the ways in which people with dementia are seen and treated will be more life-affirming and life-enhancing. There is the hope that as we understand more about processes of communication and the nature of symbolism, so it will be possible for people with dementia and their carers to communicate for much longer on many more issues. And ultimately, there is the hope that eventually we shall find ways of preventing the spread of these various diseases and that dementia may become a thing of the past.

To do all this requires great commitment of course. Commitment of work. Commitment of people, and commitment of resources. In a society where there are so many conflicting demands upon what are considered to be scarce resources, we have to ask where in the pecking order do we find, and do we wish to find, our resolve to improve the situation of people with dementia and their carers. That is ultimately a political question. As Jacques (1997) points out, our good intentions and commitment:

> can founder on the rocks of inadequate funding, inadequate resources and lack of political will, which have to be partly put down to public indifference to the plight

of some of the most vulnerable people in our communities.

It is also an ethical and a theological problem. One which forces us to explore the social, economic and political dimension of our faith statements. As people live longer and more people require treatment and support from our health services; as the number of people with dementia grows – so the cost escalates and creates a real and identifiable economic and political challenge. We are perhaps being forced to ask what sort of society we wish to live in and what are the guiding principles that we wish to affirm. It may be that the vote-winning 'cut taxes' is not necessarily the principle which most reflects our Christian understanding.

Lord as we hold before you people with dementia
We are confronted by mystery and sadness,
by ambiguity and confusion.

We pray for all who are engaged in research
looking for ways to prevent or slow down this condition, and
We pray for all who seek to provide
imaginative and creative patterns and structures of caring.

May all who live with this disability
find that they are understood and supported,
cherished and cared for, and
may those who look on, and endeavour
to stand alongside them, find encouragement and strength.

We give thanks that people with dementia
remain accepted and loved by you, and
We ask that their souls may be
nourished and enlightened by the
presence and power of your Spirit.

Chapter 13
Epilogue

We'll give a voice to those who have not spoken
We'll find the words for those whose lips are sealed,
We'll make the tunes for those who sing no longer
Vibrating love alive in every heart.
We'll share our joy with those who still are weeping
Chant hymns of strength for hearts that break in grief
We'll leap and dance the resurrection story
Including all within the circles of our love.
June Boyce-Tillman

Whenever I sing this hymn in church I find myself debating with myself as to whether it is true in relation to people with dementia. I would so like it to be! I have kept it to the last section of this book to quote because it is so positive, so vibrant and hopeful. And that is what I would like the whole world of dementia care to be.

In my opening chapter I wrote about the experience of the Exile for the children of Israel. How their beautiful city of Jerusalem had been ransacked, their Temple burned down and many of their number marched away, hundreds of miles, into the foreign land of Babylonia. There, in a strange land, they had to discover how to live together in peace and harmony, how to re-think their religious understanding and discover a new hope. Most of them would not return to Judah, they would spend the rest of their days in this foreign land, and the challenge was to discover how to live there with creativity and hope.

This they were able to do and some of the most beautiful chapters in the Bible now bear testimony to that new experience. The so-called 'servant songs' in Isaiah[32] bear witness to a new understanding of the nature of suffering, of the experience of vulnerability and the all-encompassing love and mercy of God. From the ashes of destruction there bloomed a new flower of hope.

So is there any further hope, any other good news, for people with dementia, beyond that outlined in the previous chapter?

Yes, there is the good news that they are loved and accepted by God in ways that we may never understand nor be able to express. This love is not dependent upon their memory, upon their goodness, upon their moral rectitude or upon their believing or their unbelieving. It is a gift, sheer grace, and is wholly and utterly unconditional. It is a love that will never let them go and which will accompany them through the ravages of their illness and through the mystery of death. It is a love that has been there, often unrecognised, from the very beginning, and it will remain with them until the very end.

If we have no good news for the person with dementia then surely we have very little good news to offer anyone else. We are being invited to walk into a new phase of experiencing and understanding God. It is one in which we are always the receiver. We are the blessed and the accepted, and nothing is required of us save that we are ourselves – just as we are. And that is enough. That is always enough. There is a fullness of spirituality for the person with dementia and never let it be said that the churches or communities of faith denied or hindered that truth.

I have written elsewhere (Goldsmith 2001) about the sheer audacity of this gospel:

---

[32] Isaiah 42v1-4; 49v1-6; 50v4-9; 52v13-53v12.

What sort of good news is it that requires us to take the initiative? What sort of Gospel is it that expects us to earn our salvation through acts of belief – for surely the word *'earn'* is appropriate if our salvation ultimately depends upon an act that *we* take.

But if God's gift and love extends to all, irrespective of their understanding or their memory; irrespective of their worthiness or their faithfulness – then we have quite a Gospel on our hands! But beware: it is I a Gospel that offends all those who regard their own profession of faith as somehow being an integral part of that salvation story. It offends those who like to draw circles that allow some people to be on the inside and regard others as being on the outside. It offends those who feel that there are some people who have created a great gulf between themselves and God which will only be breached by some action on the part of the estranged . . . but what if that action has already been taken? What if one who has been estranged, has stooped down to enfold the whole of humanity, and what if already the outcast and the marginalised, the confused and the bewildered, the healthy and the sick, the righteous and the unrighteous, the repentant and the unrepentant – what if they have all been received and welcomed, loved and forgiven by a gracious God who permits no barriers of ignorance, sinfulness or sickness to deflect his loving purposes, now that would be good news! . . . .

And isn't this precisely the challenge that dementia raises? For I firmly believe that each and every person with dementia is loved and accepted and enfolded by God; not because of *their* faithfulness but because of God's faithfulness.

It is our responsibility and privilege to be the ambassadors of this message of hope. It must be embedded not only in our words but also in our actions and in our ways of thinking.

> O Lord, support us all the day long of this troublous life, until the shades lengthen, and the evening comes, and the busy world is hushed, the fever of life is over, and our work is done. Then, Lord, in thy mercy, grant us safe lodging, a holy rest, and peace at the last; through Jesus Christ our Lord.[33]

---

[33] From the Book of Common Prayer

Appendix A
Form of service to be used
on admittance to a nursing home

We meet here today to mark a new stage in the life of N as he/she moves into a new home in (name of nursing home).

We meet to give thanks to God for all the benefits and blessings that N has received over the years, and to pray that he/she may be conscious of the continuing presence of God in this room and in this home.

Let us remember the words of the psalmist, reflecting on the fact that wherever we may be, we never stray beyond the boundaries of God's loving care. Words from Psalm 139 (v 1-18):

O Lord, thou hast searched me out, and known me:
thou knowest my down-sitting, and mine up-rising; thou understandest my thoughts long before.

Thou art about my path, and about my bed:
and spiest out all my ways.

For lo, there is not a word in my tongue:
but thou, O Lord, knowest it altogether.

Thou hast fashioned me behind and before:
and laid thine hand upon me.

Such knowledge is too wonderful and excellent for me:
I cannot attain unto it.

Whither shall I go then from thy Spirit:
or whither shall I go then from thy presence?

If I climb up to heaven, thou art there:
if I go down to hell, thou art there also.

If I take the wings of the morning:
and remain in the uttermost parts of the sea;

Even there also shall thy hand lead me:
and thy right hand shall hold me.

If I say, Peradventure the darkness shall cover me:
then shall my night be turned to day.

Yea, the darkness is no darkness with thee, but the night is as clear as the day:
the darkness and light to thee are both alike.

For my reins are thine:
thou hast covered me in my mother's womb

I will give thanks unto thee, for I am fearfully and wonderfully made:
marvellous are thy works, and that my soul knoweth right well.

My bones are not hid from thee:
though I be made secretly, and fashioned beneath in the earth.

Thine eyes did see my substance, yet being imperfect:
and in thy book were all my members written.

Which day by day were fashioned;
when as yet there were none of them.

How dear are thy counsels unto me, O God:
O how great is the sum of them!

If I tell them, they are more in number than the sand;
When I wake up I am present with thee.[34]

And now we remember how Jesus sent his disciples out with the promise that he would remain with them. Matthew's Gospel records him as saying: "I am with you always, even unto the end of the world".

We gain strength and comfort from these assurances in scripture and we pray that N may find them to be true in his/her experiences here, in this new place.

We pray for the staff here, and for all who will care for and befriend N. those who will prepare his/her meals, deal with his/her laundry and for all who will provide friendship, conversation, stimulation, support and relief.

---

[34] From the Book of Common Prayer

As we look ahead into an unknown future, so we give thanks for the fact that we are still your disciples and that you still have work for us, wherever we are, no matter what our circumstances.

Help N to fill his/her time with thoughts of you, with a desire for your grace and with opportunities to reflect on and bask in your merciful love and acceptance.

We recall the words of Jesus when he taught his followers about the nature of the godly life, from the mountainside beside the Sea of Galilee

Blessed are the poor in spirit: for theirs is the kingdom of heaven.
Blessed are they that mourn: for they shall be comforted.
Blessed are the meek: for they shall inherit the earth.
Blessed are they which do hunger and thirst after righteousness: for they shall be filled.
Blessed are the merciful: for they shall obtain mercy.
Blessed are the pure in heart: for they shall see God.
Blessed are the peacemakers: for they shall be called the children of God
. . (So) let your light shine before men, that they may see your good works and glorify your Father which is in heaven.[35] (Matthew 5 v3-9 & v16)

(Now let us remember X, Y & Z – N's family and friends at this time . .
. . and recall any special items for prayer . . .)

We join together in the Lord's Prayer . . ..

Finally, two prayers from the ancient service of Compline:[36]

Visit, we beseech thee, O Lord, this place, and drive far from it all the snares of the enemy; let thy holy angels dwell herein to preserve u in peace; and may thy blessing be upon us evermore, through Jesus Christ our Lord. Amen

Be present, O merciful God, and protect us through the silent hours (of night-time), so that we who are wearied by the changes and chances of this fleeting world, may repose upon thy eternal changelessness. Amen

The Blessing

---

[35] From the Authorised Version
[36] From the Book of Common Prayer with the additions and deviations proposed in 1928

Appendix B
A service of remembrance and thanksgiving for friends and family of people with dementia in residential care

The intention behind this service is to bring together relatives and friends of people with dementia who are now in a nursing or who may have been resident there before they died. It is suggested that the service be held every six months and that a letter is sent out to relatives beforehand. If possible, it should take place within the nursing home itself. The service is not primarily for the residents – other (weekly? monthly?) services are held for them. However, if residents wish to attend, then clearly they should be welcomed, but the content of the service is unashamedly structured with relatives and friends in mind.

People attending the service could be invited to write the name of their relative or friend on a card, and the cards could be collected at the beginning of the service, placed in a basket and placed upon the altar/table or focal point. A visible sign of the invisible love and care represented by all the people attending. Some people might like to invite people to come forward at some stage in the service and place the cards in the basket then.

What follows is very much a draft – giving possible ideas. It will need to be adapted for the particular people and place that you have in mind.

Call to Worship
The prophet Isaiah writes about God's love for his people, and for the city of Jerusalem which had been destroyed by the Babylonian army – he writes

> Can a woman forget the infant at her breast,
> or a loving mother the child of her womb?
> Even these forget, yet I will not forget you,
> I have engraved you upon the palms of my hands [37]

---

[37] Isaiah 49 v 15-16

We meet together in this place to remember that continuing love of God; to gain strength and comfort from the knowledge that His love continues even when there is devastation all around. We meet and rejoice in the fact that there is no place which is beyond the love and mercy of God, and no person who is not loved and accepted by God, whatever their condition.

Opening Hymn
>Be still for the presence of the Lord
>OR some other hymn which reminds people of the presence of God.

An Act of Reflection
We have come together to remember before God our family members and friends whose lives have been diminished by their experience of illness. Whose memories have faded, and whose breadth of experience has become so limited. We acknowledge the pain and hurt that we feel having lost some aspects of the relationships that we shared with them.

But we give thanks for their lives, for all their achievements, for all their interests and activities, for their work and their concerns. We recall their lives with pride and know that the richness of their living will continue in our hearts and minds, and in the memory and love of God.

We come to acknowledge our own sense of confusion and inadequacy , our experience of powerlessness and sometimes of anger in the face of these illnesses which seem to creep up on us from nowhere and take away our loved ones from us.

We give thanks for the professional and sensitive care that is available within the community, and for all the people who have helped us to sustain our relationships and who have supported us in our times of darkness. We give thanks for this place, and for those who work in it.

And we symbolise our love and our concern, our friendship and our ongoing commitment to those who are ill, by placing before God their names, recognising that each name represents a lifetime of loving and relating, of laughter and of work.

(as the names are brought forward, music may be played – and a sense of calm and well-being should be encouraged)

A Time for Silence
In a few moments of quietness, let us remember before God, the person that we have in our hearts at this time. Let us remember the good times we have shared . . . . . and the times of difficulty . . . . we remember the times when we have laughed and the times when we have cried . . . . .

We remember holidays we have shared, and special places we have visited . . . . .

We remember other members of our families, and all who are affected by this present illness . . . . .

Let us remember all who have died, those people who have filled our life with meaning and purpose, with radiance and with joy . . . . .

(a time of silence)

Let us share with God, those things which we would want to share with those who are ill – all the things that we would like to say to them – and let us pray that in God's own mysterious way, the burden of our hearts may be communicated in ways beyond our understanding.

A Time of Sorrow and a Time of Hope
The Psalmist said
> Why are you so full of heaviness, my soul
> and why are you so disquieted within me?
> O put your trust in God
> for I will praise him yet who is my deliverer and my God[38]

We bring before God our sorrow, and we look to God for strength and consolation, for hope and for a belief that there can be life and times of joy again, despite the sadness of this time.

We entrust our loved ones into the care of this home; grateful for the safety and the continuing care and support that they receive.

---

[38] Psalm 43 v6-7

We return to our homes; we continue to pray for all who are here, whether as residents or staff. We want this home to be a place of loving refreshment, and we ask that God's Spirit may abide here always.

Hymn
> The Lord's my shepherd OR When I survey

Blessing.

NOTE

A service such as this needs to be prepared with great care and should involve discussion with colleagues and, if possible, with staff members in the home. It needs to be designed specifically for the people involved. Perhaps there can be readings, from scripture, or of different kinds of verse. Maybe some of the people involved could be encouraged to write their own pieces or special prayers.

I am very conscious that I can do no more here than give an indication of what might be designed, and to suggest that people think along these lines and ensure that this particular experience of living and dying is somehow remembered and hallowed in a particular way.

Appendix C
Model letter of agreement between a church and a nursing home.

St John's Church   Sea View Nursing Home
Main Street   Harbour Road
Anytown   Anytown
Phone: 1234   *Phone:5678*

The clergy and members of St John's Church, working under the direction of the *Rector* and with the agreement of the *Manager* agree to provide pastoral and spiritual care to the residents of Sea View Nursing Home, should they wish this.

St John's is an *Anglican/Presbyterian/Baptist* church, but approaches this work in an ecumenical spirit, and is willing to try put people in touch with their own church if they would like this.

The church will endeavour to hold a service every *Sunday afternoon at 3pm* at which residents and their friends and family are welcome.

Holy Communion will be brought to residents by arrangement, and the *Rector* is willing to visit any resident on request. He/She is willing to respond to any urgent calls for pastoral care of patients, families or staff at any time. The church may also be called upon for any help in arranging funeral or memorial services.

Sea View Nursing Home will endeavour to welcome and support the ministry of St John's Church in this work.

The *Rector* and *Manager* agree to meet up every three months to discuss this working arrangement, which may be terminated by either party at any time.

References

Airy J, et al (2002) *Frequently asked questions on Spirituality and Religion* published by the Sheffield Churches Council for Community Care; Faith in Elderly People, Leeds; MHA Care Group; and the Christian Council on Ageing.

Allen K (1994) *Dementia in acute units: wandering* in 'Nursing Standard 9, 8

Allen K (2001) *Communication and Consultation* Joseph Rowntree Foundation, The Policy Press, Bristol

Archibald C (1994) *Sex: is it a problem?* in 'Journal of Dementia Care' July/August - and - *Never too late to fall in love* in 'Journal of Dementia Care', Sept/October (1997) *Sexuality and Dementia?* in 'State of the art in dementia care' Ed Marshall M, Centre for Policy on Ageing

AS-AD (2003) *Don't make the journey alone – a message from fellow travellers* Alzheimer Scotland – Action of Dementia

AS-AD (2003b) *Signposts to Support: Understanding the special needs of carers of people with dementia* Alzheimer Scotland-Action on Dementia (22 Drumsheugh Gardens, Edinburgh EH3 7RN)

AS-GB (1994) *Home Alone: living alone with dementia* Alzheimer's Society, London

AS-GB (2000) *Living Alone: advice leaflet* Alzheimer's Society, London

Baker JA (1976) *Travels in Oudamovia* Faith Press, Leighton Buzzard

Barker G & Wattis J (1991) *Dangerous Liaisons?* in 'Nursing the Elderly' March/ April

Barton J, Grudzen M, & Zielske R (2003) *Vital Connections in Long-Term Care; Spiritual Resources for Staff and Residents'* Health Professions Press, Baltimore

Bayer, A (2001) *Drugs to treat Alzheimer's Disease Present and Future* in 'Signpost' Vol 5 No 3, February 2001

Bayley J (1998) *Iris – a memoir of Iris Murdoch* Duckworth, London (later issued by Abacus)

Bayley J (1999) *Iris and the Friends* Duckworth, London (later Abacus)

Bayley J (2001) *Widower's House* Duckworth, London (later Abacus)

Bender M & Cheston R (1997) *Inhabitants of a lost kingdom: A model of the subjective Experiences of dementia* in 'Ageing and Society 17, 513-532

Boden C (1998) *Who will I be when I die?* Harper Collins (Australia) East Melbourne

Bright R (1997) *Wholeness in Later Life* Jessica Kingsley, London

Bryden C (2002) D*ementia – A Spiritual Journey Towards the Divine: A Personal View of Dementia* in "Mental Health and Spirituality in Later Life" Ed. Elizabeth MacKinlay, Haworth Pastoral Press, Binghampton N.Y.

Buber M (1958) *I and Thou,* translated by Ronald Gregor Smith, Charles Scribners' Sons, New York

Burns A & Rabins P (2000) *Carer burden in dementia* in 'The International Journal of Geriatric Psychiatry' July 15 Suppl 1 S9-13

Cantes S & Rigby P (1997) *Freedom to wander safely* in 'Elderly Care' 9 (4) 8-10

Carpentier N & Ducharme F (2003) *Caregiver network transformations: the need for an Integrated perspective* in ' Ageing and Society' Vol 23 Part 4 July 2003

Cassidy S (1988) *Sharing the Darkness* Darton Longman & Todd, London

Cheston R & Bender M (1999) *Understanding Dementia – the man with worried eyes* Jessica Kingsley Publishers, London

Clare J (1997) *John Clare* Everyman's Poetry Ed. RKR Thornton, JM Dent, London

Clare L (2002) *We'll fight it as long as we can: coping with the onset of Alzheimer's disease* in 'Aging & Mental Health 6 (2) 139-148

Clarke R (2003) *A sacred space: communicating with my mother* in Issue 9, Sept 2003 Newsletter of The Leveson Centre for the study of Ageing, Spirituality and Social Policy

Cobb M (2001) *Spiritual Care at the end of life* Open University Press

Cohen D (1991) *The subjective experience of Alzheimer's disease: the Anatomy of an illness as perceived by patients and families* in 'American Journal of Alzheimer's Care and Related Disorders and Research' May/June 1991

Cooper B et al (1995) *The prevalence of depression in the carers of dementia sufferers* in 'The International Journal of Geriatric Psychiatry' 10; 237-242

Cotrell V & Schulz R (1993) *The perspective of the patient with Alzheimer's disease: A neglected dimension of dementia research* in 'The Gerontologist' 33, 205

Coulson I (1993) *The impact of the total environment in the care and management of dementia* in 'American Journal of Alzheimer's Care and Related Disorders and Research', May/June 18-25

Crisp J (1995) *Making sense of the stories that people with Alzheimer's tell: a journey with my mother* in 'Nursing Enquiry' 2.3

Crisp J (2000) *Keeping in Touch with someone who has Alzheimer's* Ausmed Publications, Melbourne

Crisp J (2003) *Communication* in 'Dementia Nursing: A Guide to Practice' Ed. Rosalie Hudson, Ausmed, Melbourne

Davies S & Nolan M (2003) *Making the best of things: relatives' experiences of decisions about care-home entry* in 'Ageing and Society' Vol 23 Part 4 July 2003

Davis R (1987) *My Journey into Alzheimer's Disease* Scripture Press, Amersham, Buckinghamshire

De Baggio T (2002) *Losing My Mind: An Intimate Look at Life with Alzheimer's* The Free Press, New York

Derouesne C et al (1996) *Sexual behavioural changes in Alzheimer's disease* in 'Alzheimer Disease and Associated Disorders' 10 (2)

De Vugt et al (2003) *Behavioural disturbances in dementia patients and the Quality of the marital relationship* in 'International Journal of Geriatric Psychiatry' Vol 18 No 2

Downs M et al (2002) *How can we improve GPs' response to dementia* in 'Journal of Dementia Care' Vol 10 No 3 May/June

English J (1979) *What do grown up children owe their parents* in 'Having Children; Philosophical and Legal Reflections on Parenthood' Eds. O'Neill O & Ruddick W, OUP London

Everett D (2000) *Spiritual care: stretching the soul* in 'Journal of Dementia Care' 8 (1) January/February 2000

Fearnley K et al (1997) *The Right to Know? Sharing the diagnosis of dementia* Alzheimer Scotland – Action on Dementia

Fontana A & Smith R (1989) *Alzheimer's disease victims: the 'unbecoming' of self and the normalisation of competence* in 'Sociological Perspectives, 32, 1

Ford A (2003) *They also serve: Home Care of the chronically ill* in 'The Gerontologist' Vol 43 No 3 June 2003

Froggatt A (1994) *Tuning in to meet spiritual needs* in 'The Journal of Dementia Care' March/April 1994

Furlong M (1974) *God's a good man* Mowbrays, London and Oxford

Gibran, K (1926) *The Prophet* Heinemann Ltd, London

Gibson F (1999) *Can we risk person-centred communication?* In 'Journal of Dementia Care' Sept/Oct 1999

Gill A (2003) in 'The Sunday Times' Magazine, March 2 2003

Gillies B (1995) *The subjective experience of dementia: a qualitative analysis of interviews with dementia sufferers and their carers, and the implications for service provision* Joint Information and Research Group, Tayside Health Board and Tayside Regional Social Work Department

Goldsmith M (1994) *A voice from the base of the pyramid* in 'Journal of Dementia Care July/Aug 1994

Goldsmith M (1996) *Hearing the Voice of People with Dementia* Jessica Kingsley Publishers, London

Goldsmith M (1999) *Ethical Issues in Dementia Care* in 'Dementia Care: Developing Partnerships in Practice' Eds Adams T & Clarke C, Bailiere Tindall, London

Goldsmith M (1999b) *Dementia: A Challenge to Christian Theology and Pastoral Care* in 'Spirituality and Ageing' Ed. A Jewell, Jessica Kingsley Publishers, London

Goldsmith M (2001) *Through a glass darkly: a dialogue between dementia and faith* in 'Aging, Spirituality and Pastoral Care' Eds MacKinlay, Ellor & Pickard, The Haworth Pastoral Press, Binghampton NY

Goldsmith M (2003) *Intimacy* in 'Dementia Nursing - a Guide to Practice Ed. Rosalie Hudson, Ausmed, Melbourne

Goodall M (1999) *Worshipping with those who have dementia* in 'Spirituality and Ageing' Ed. A Jewell, Jessica Kingsley, London

Grant L (1998) *Remind me who I am again* Granta Books, London

Grey (1994) *The Spiritual Component of Palliative Care* in 'Palliative Medicine' 8 p215-21, quoted in Cobb (2001)

Grudzen M (2003) *The Face of Dignity: Honouring the Individuality of Residents and Staff* in 'Vital Connections in Long-Term Care; Spiritual Resources for Staff and Residents' Eds Barton, Grudzen & Zielske Health Professions Press, Baltimore

Gwyther, L (1995) *You are one of us* Duke University Medical Centre, USA

Haddad P & Benbow S (1993) *Sexual problems associated with dementia: Part 1 – Problems and their consequences* in 'International Journal of Geriatric Psychiatry' Vol 8 547-551

Hammond G (2002) *The Memory Box* published by Faith in Elderly People Leeds; 29 Silverdale Avenue, Leeds LS20 8BD

Helen (1994) Printed in the July magazine of the Alzheimer's Association (USA), the Cleveland Area Chapter

Henderson C & Andrews N (1998) *Partial View; An Alzheimer's Journal* Southern Methodist University Press, Dallas

Heston L & White J (1991) *The vanishing mind: A practical guide to Alzheimer's Disease and other dementias* Freeman, New York

Hide K (2002) *Symbol Ritual and Dementia* in 'Mental Health and Spirituality in Later Life' Ed MacKinlay E, Haworth Pastoral Press, Binghampton, NY
Hughes J (2003) *Don't tuck me in* in 'The Tablet' 5 July 2003
Ignatieff M (1993) *Scar Tissue* Vintage Books, London
Innes A, et al (2003) *Dementia services in remote and rural areas* in 'Journal of Dementia Care' Vol 11 No.4 July/Aug 2003
Ison, J (1998) *A Tapestry of Lives* in 'Aging and Religion' 2 Feb (1-8)
Jackson G & MacDonald C (2003) *Aggression* in 'Dementia Nursing: A Guide to Practice' Ed. Rosalie Hudson, Ausmed, Melbourne
Jacques A (1992) *Understanding Dementia (second edition)* Churchill Livingstone, Edinburgh & London
Jacques A (1997) *Ethical Dilemmas in Care and Research for People with Dementia* in 'Dementia Challenges and New Directions: Research Highlights in Social Work 31 Ed. S Hunter, Jessica Kingsley, London
Jansen V (1999) *Alzheimer's: the Good, the Sad and the Humorous* Published privately ISBN 0-9672563-0-5
Jenkins D (2004) *Geriatric Burden or Elderly Blessing?* In 'Ageing, Spirituality and Well-being' Ed A Jewell, Jessica Kingsley Publishers, London
Jeremiah M (2003) *Alone with Dementia* published privately, obtainable from 43 Boat Dyke Road, Upton, Norwich NR13 6BL
Kantrowitz B (1989) *Trapped inside her own world* in 'Newsweek' Dec 18th
Keady J & Gilliard J (1999) *The early exprience of Alzheimer's disease: implications for partnership and practice* in 'Dementia Care: Developing Partnerships in Practice' Eds. Adams & Clarke Bailliere Tindall, London
Keady J & Nolan M (1994) *Younger onset dementia: developing a longitudinal model as the basis for a research agenda and as a guide to interventions with sufferers and carers* in 'Journal of Advanced Nursing' 19, 659-669
Keady J, Nolan M & Gilliard J (1995) *Listen to the voices of experience* in 'Journal of Dementia Care' May/June

Keck D (1996) *Forgetting whose we are: Alzheimer's Disease and the Love of God,* Abingdon Press, Nashville

Killick J (1997a) 'The Barrow' in *You are Words* Hawker Publications Ltd, London

Killick J (1997a2) 'The Naming Game' in op cit

Killick J (1997b) *Communication: a matter of the life and death of the Mind* in 'Journal of Dementia Care' vol 5 no. 5

Killick J (2000) *Openings: dementia poems and photographs,* Hawker Publications, London

Kimble, M (2002) *The Defiant Power of the Human Spirit; Mental Health in Later Life* in 'Mental Health and Spirituality in Later Life' Ed MacKinlay E, Haworth Pastoral Press, Binghampton, NY

Kinsey Bambery J (1997) *Spirituality as a healing force* in 'Spirituality – the Heart of Nursing' Ed. S Richardson, Ausmed, Melbourne

Kitwood T (1990) *The dialectics of dementia: with particular reference to Alzheimer's disease* in 'Ageing & Society' 10, 177-196

Kitwood T (1990b) *Psychotherapy and Dementia* in BPS Psychotherapy Section newsletter 8

Kitwood T (1997) *Personhood, dementia and dementia care* in 'Research Highlights in Social Work 31: Dementia – Challenges and New Directions' Ed. Susan Hunter, Jessica Kingsley Publishers, London

Kitwood T (1997b) *Dementia Reconsidered: The person comes first* Open University Press, Buckingham

Koenig H (1994) *Aging and God; Spiritual pathways to Mental Health in Midlife and Later Years* The Haworth Press, Binghampton

Kubler Ross E (1970) *On Death and Dying* Tavistock, London

Kushner H (1981) *When bad things happen to good people* Pan Books, London

Lai C & Arthur D (2003) *Wandering* in 'Dementia Nursing: A Guide to Practice' Ed. Rosalie Hudson Ausmed, Melbourne

Lawrence R (2003) *Aspects of Spirituality in dementia care* in 'Dementia: The International Journal of Social Research and Practice Vol 2 No 3 October 2003

Lee J (2003)? *Just Love me: My life turned upside down by Alzheimer's disease* Purdue University Press, West Lafayette, Indiana

Lewinsohn P et al (1991) *Age and depression: unique and shared effects* in 'Psychology and Ageing' 6, 247-260

Litz B et al (1989) *Sexual concerns of male partners of female Alzheimer disease patients* in 'The Gerontologist' 30, 1 113-116

Lively P (1987) *Moon Tiger* Andre Deutsch, London

Lubinski R (1991) *Dementia and Communication* Decker, London

McGowin D (1993) *Living in the Labyrinth: A personal journey through the Maze of Alzheimer's* Elder Books, San Francisco

McKee, K (1999) *This is Your Life: research paradigms in dementia care* in 'Dementia Care: Developing Partnerships in Practice Eds Adams & Clarke Bailliere Tindall, London

Mace N & Rabins P (1981) *The 36 Hour Day,* Age Concern and Hodder & Stoughton, London

McGregor I & Bell J (1994) *Buzzing with life, energy and drive* in 'Journal of Dementia Care' 2, 6

Miller J (1990) *Goodbye to all this in* 'Independent on Sunday: Sunday Review, 15 April

Miller S (2003) *The Story of My Father* Bloomsbury Publishing plc

Mistry R (2002) *Family Matters* Faber and Faber, London

Moore V (2003) *Dementia Care Mapping* in 'Dementia Nursing – a Guide to Practice' Ed. Rosalie Hudson, Ausmed Publications, Melbourne

Murphy C (1994) *It started with a Sea-Shell: Life Story Work and People with Dementia* Dementia Services Development Centre, the University of Stirling

Murphy C & Moyes M (1997) *Life Story Work* in 'State of the art in dementia care' Ed. Mary Marshall, Centre for Policy on Ageing (CPA)

Pitkeathley J (1989) *It's my duty, isn't it? The plight of carers in our Society* Souvenir Press, London

Rau M (1993)   *Coping with communication challenges in Alzheimer's Disease,* Singular Publishing Group, San Diego CA

Russell M (2001) *Listening to dementia. A new paradigm for theology?* In 'Contact' 135 p13-21

Sacks J (2002) *'Spirituality' is escapist, shallow and self-indulgent* in 'The Times' August 24th 2002

Sacks O (1985) *The man who mistook his wife for a hat* Picador/Pan books

Sarton M (1983) *As We Are Now* The Women's Press, Ltd

Schweitzer A (1910) *The Quest of the Historical Jesus* A & C Black Ltd, London

Seeber J (2001) *Pastoral Support for Late-Life Sexuality* in 'Aging, Spirituality and Pastoral Care' Eds MacKinlay et al The Haworth Pastoral Press, Binghampton, NY

Shamy E (2003) *A Guide to the Spiritual Dimension of Care for People with Alzheimer's Disease and Related Dementia* Jessica Kingsley, London. Originally Published in 1997 as *More than Body, Brain and Breath* ColCom Press, Orewa, Aotearoa – New Zealand

Sheild R (1997) *Liminality in an American Nursing Home: the endless transition* in 'The Cultural Context of Aging' Ed. Sokolorsky J, Bergin & Garvey, Westport CT (Quoted by Sharon Waller in her paper *'Liminality in Late Life'*)

Sherman B (1998) *Sex, Intimacy and Aged Care* Jessica Kingsley, London

Sinason V (1992) *Mental Handicap and the Human Condition* Free Association Books, London

Snowdon D (2001) *Aging with Grace* Fourth Estate, Harper Collins, London

Sommers C (1986) *Filial Morality* in 'Journal of Philosophy' 83, 438-456

Stoter D (1995) *Spiritual Aspects of Health Care* Mosby, London

Swinton J (2001) *Spirituality and Mental Health Care* Jessica Kingsley, London

Thiselton A   (1986) *Language Liturgy and Meaning*   Grove Liturgical Study No.2 Grove Books Ltd. Nottingham

Treetops J (1996) *Holy, Holy, Holy. The Church's ministry with people with dementia: suggestions for action* Faith in Elderly People Project, c/o 53 Cardigan Lane, Leeds LS4 2LE

Waller S (2002) *Dementia as Culture* An unpublished paper, quoted with permission

Waller S (2002b) *Dementia and Meaning: Evolution of a Cultural Construction* an unpublished paper, quoted by permission

Walton J (1999) *Young Onset Dementia* in 'Dementia Care-Developing Partnerships in Practice' Eds. Adams T & Clarke C, Bailliere Tindall, London

Ward R (2000) *Waiting to be heard – dementia and the gay community* In 'Journal of Dementia Care' 8 (3) 24-25

Webber L (1994) Quoted in 'Ageing and God: Spiritual Pathways to Mental Health in Midlife and Later Years' by Harold Koenig The Haworth Press

Wenger G (2001) *Myths and realities of ageing in rural Britain* in 'Ageing and Society' 21, 117-130

Whalley L (1997) *Early Onset Dementia* in 'Dementia – Challenges and New Directions. Research Highlights in Social Work 31

Whitworth A et al (1999) *Communication in dementia care: a partnership approach* in 'Dementia Care – Developing Partnerships in Practice' Eds. Adams T & Clarke C, Bailliere Tindall, London Ed. Susan Hunter, Jessica Kingsley Publications

Woods R (1989) *Alzheimer's disease: Coping with a living death* Souvenir Press, London

Woods R (1997) *Why should family caregivers feel guilty?* in 'The State of Art in Dementia Care' Ed. Marshall M, Centre for Policy on Ageing, London

Yancy P (2001) *Where is God when it hurts?* Multnomah Press

AUTHOR INDEX

INDEX